With Harp and Lute

With Harp and Lute

By
Blanche Jennings Thompson

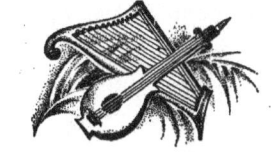

Illustrations by Kate Seredy

Hillside Education

Hillside Education © 2024

Originally published by The Macmillan Company, 1935

All rights reserved. No part of this publication may be reproduced in whole or in part, stored in a retrieval system or transmitted in any form or by any means, electronic, mechanical, photocopying, recording, or otherwise, without prior written permission of the publisher.

Cover Image: *Virgin and Child with Four Angels* by Gerard David
Public Domain, National Gallery of Art Open Access

Cover and interior book design by Mary Jo Loboda

ISBN: 978-1-955402-18-7

Hillside Education
475 Bidwell Hill Road
Lake Ariel, PA 18436
www.hillsideeducation.com

Give praise unto the Lord upon the harp, upon the harp and with voice of psalms, with the long trumpets, and the sound of the cornet.

The root of Jesse hath budded, a star hath arisen out of Jacob; a virgin hath borne the Saviour. We praise Thee, O our God.

In honour of this most chaste virgin, let us sing canticles with sweet harmony.

Acknowledgments

Thanks are due to the publishers and authors listed below, by and with whose permission the enumerated copyrighted selections are included.

To *The Commonweal* for "Contrition Across the Waves" by Caroline Giltinan; "Ad Matrem in Caelis" by Charles L. O'Donnell, C. S. C.

To *Spirit* for "Ad Mariam" by Sister M. Edwardine, O. M.; "Little Serenade" by Kenton Kilmer; "Ash Wednesday" by Rosa Zagnoni Marinoni.

To *America* for "Wealth," "The Welcome," "The Lonely Crib," "The Way of the Cross," "A Gift of Flowers," "Nails" by Leonard Feeney, S. J.

To *The Sign* for "Mother," "A Question of Sacrifice" by Sister M. Eulalia, R. S. M.

To *The Torch* for "The Knights" by Sister Maryanna, O. P.

To *Magnificat* for "Gifts" by Sister Mary of the Visitation.

To Charles Scribner's Sons for "A Ballad of Trees and the Master" by Sidney Lanier.

To Doubleday, Doran & Company for "Ambition" by Aline Kilmer; "Multiplication," "Kings" by Joyce Kilmer; "The Mother of Judas" by Amelia Josephine Burr.

To the Viking Press for "Christmas Morning" by Elizabeth Madox Roberts.

To Dodd, Mead & Company for "The Christ Child" by Gilbert K. Chesterton.

To Scott, Foresman and Company for "Johneen" by Patrick J. Carroll, C. S. C.

To Remington, Putnam Company for "The Good Joan" by Lizette Woodworth Reese.

To the Robert M. McBride Company for "Our Lord and Our Lady" by Hilaire Belloc.

To The Macmillan Company for "Sheep and Lambs," "Man of the House" by Katherine Tynan Hinkson; "Grace for Light" by Moira O'Neill; "Ballad of Father Gilligan" by William Butler Yeats; "To the Lighted Lady Window" by Marguerite Wilkinson; "A Cradle Song" by Padraic Colum; selections from the *Catholic Anthology* by Thomas Walsh.

To P. J. Kenedy & Sons for translations of liturgical poems from *Blessed Be God* by Rev. Chas. J. Callan, O. P. and Rev. John A. McHugh, O. P.

To Benziger Bros, for liturgical poems from *The Roman Missal, My Prayer Book* by Rev. F. X. Lasance; "Resignation" by Mother Francis D'Assisi, O. S. U.

To Ginn and Company for "Madonna Remembers" by Sister M. Edwardine from *The Rosary Readers, Book VI.*

To The Catholic Encyclopedia, Inc. for "The Housewife's Prayer" from *The Valley of Vision* by Blanche Mary Kelly.

To Alfred A. Knopf Company for "Spiritism" from *Collected Poems* by Robert Hillyer.

To D. Appleton-Century Company for "The Spinning Top" from *Starshine and Candlelight* by Sister Mary Angelita, B. V. M.

To the Bruce Publishing Company for "October of the Angels" by James J. Daly, S. J.

To Longmans, Green & Company for "Ad Matrem in Caelis" by Charles L. O'Donnell, C. S. C.

Acknowledgments

The gratitude of the author is also due to the following for personal permission to use poems written or owned by them:

Amelia Josephine Burr for "The Mother of Judas."

Sister M. Madeleva, C. S. C. for "Christmas in Provence."

Sister M. Eleanore, C. S. C. for "The Missionary" and "The Vocation of St. Francis."

Sister M. Edwardine, O. M. for "Madonna Remembers" and "Ad Mariam."

Sister Mariella, O. S. B. for "The Sheep Herd."

Sister Mary Eulalia, R. S. M. for "Mother" and "A Question of Sacrifice."

Sister Albertus Magnus, O. P. for "A Prayer."

Sister Mary of the Visitation for "Gifts."

Mother M. Columba, S. H. C. J. for "From My Window" which appeared originally in *Good Counsel*, a magazine published by The Augustinian Fathers.

Sister Teresa Marie, Dean of Nazareth College, Rochester, New York for "To Joseph" and "Answer" by Harriet Hoock.

Lillian Doherty for "Stella Matutina."

Mildred Wojtalewicz for "Sanctuary."

Rev. Leonard Feeney, S. J. for "Nails," "The Welcome," "The Lonely Crib," "The Altar Boy," "The Way of the Cross," "A Gift of Flowers."

Rev. P. J. Carroll, C. S. C. for "Johneen" from *Heart's Hermitage*.

Kenton Kilmer for "Little Serenade."

Benjamin F. Musser for "Le Coeur de l'Immaculèe" from *A Chaplet of Sanctuaries*.

Shane Leslie for versions of traditional poems appearing in his *Anthology of Catholic Poets*.

Eileen Duggan for "St. Peter."

Mother Aquinas, Bar Convent, York, England for "Rabboni! Master!" by Mother Loyola, Inst. B. V. M.

E. V. Lucas for "In Brittany" from *Playtime and Company*.

Arthur L. Pickthall for "Mary Shepherdess" from the *Lamp of Poor Souls* by Marjorie L. C. Pickthall.

Blanche Mary Kelly for "The Housewife's Prayer" from the *Valley of Vision*.

Mother Francis D'Assisi for "Resignation" from *My Candle and Other Poems*.

Lorna Gill Walsh, literary executor of Dr. Thomas Walsh, for permission to use his versions of two old Irish poems and a translation from the Spanish.

Grateful thanks are due also to Sister Mary Henry, O. P., Mr. George N. Shuster of the *Commonweal*, John Gilland Brunini, editor of *Spirit*, Rev. Patrick J. Carroll, editor of the *Ave Maria*, and Rev. Edward L. Hughes, editor of *The Torch*, for help and encouragement in various ways.

.

A Word about the Music

WITH lute, and sackbut, and psaltery in the days of old, God's sweet singers sang His holy praises. With golden strings and sounding cymbals they made "a joyful noise unto the Lord." In cloistered cells, with patient skill, the humble monks set down on parchment the words and music of the ancient chants and made them beautiful with scarlet enwrought with gold and blue in infinite variety; and even to this day in many a quiet convent gentle nuns write reverently their thoughts of God and His most holy Mother.

The Catholic child has a rich heritage in the old liturgical poetry of his church, and he should be accorded the privilege of early acquaintance with it. He should also be familiar with some, at least, of the Catholic verse appearing currently in leading publications. In addition to this somewhat restricted material, there is much poetry of interest to Catholics by writers not of their own faith. This too, should have its place in the Catholic cultural background.

It is not the purpose of this book to present to the child all of the Church's treasures—rather to open here and there a door, let him hear afar the sound of harp and lute and follow, if he will, the lovely music.

—Blanche Jennings Thompson
Franciscan Tertiary

Contents

ACKNOWLEDGMENTS I
A WORD ABOUT THE MUSIC V

FROM THE OLDEN TIMES

I SAW THREE SHIPS 2
BROWN ROBIN'S CONFESSION 3
THE FRIAR OF ORDERS GREY 5
TWO OLD LENTEN RHYMES 6
THE RUNE OF HOSPITALITY 8
THE RANN OF THE THREE 9
PRAYER BEFORE SLEEPING 9
THE BREASTPLATE OF ST. PATRICK 10
THE IRISH TE DEUM 13
A RUNE OF PRAISE 14
LAUDAMUS TE! 14
BENEDICIMUS TE! 14
ADOREMUS TE! 15
GLORIFICAMUS TE! 15

RHYMES AND RUNES

A CRADLE SONG 18
THE CHRIST-CHILD 19
OUR LORD AND OUR LADY 20
CHRISTMAS MORNING 21
LE COEUR DE L'IMMACULÉE 23
THE HOUSEWIFE'S PRAYER 24
SHEEP AND LAMBS 25
A BALLAD OF TREES AND THE MASTER 27
MAN OF THE HOUSE 28
THE MOTHER OF JUDAS 31
ST. PETER 31
ASH WEDNESDAY 33
THE GOOD JOAN 34
CONTRITION ACROSS THE WAVES 36
IN BRITTANY 37
SPIRITISM 38
THE BALLAD OF FATHER GILLIGAN 39

With Harp and Lute

The Friar	41
Grace for Light	42
Mary Shepherdess	43
Ambition	45
Multiplication	46
Kings	47
Little Serenade	48
To the Lighted Lady Window	49

From Convent Cell and Cloister

The Altar Boy	52
The Lonely Crib	53
The Welcome	54
Nails	55
A Gift of Flowers	56
The Way of the Cross	56
Ad Matrem in Caelis	57
Johneen	58
October of the Angels	60
Canticle of the Sun	61
Hymn of Love	64
To-day	65
O Jesu	66
Prayer for a Priest	67
Veni, Domine Jesu!	68
Anima Christi	69
Petitions of Saint Augustine	70
Christmas in Provence	71
The Sheep Herd	73
The Knight	74
Mother	75
A Question of Sacrifice	76
The Vocation of St. Francis	77
The Missionary	79
Resignation	80
Madonna Remembers	80
Ad Mariam	82
From My Window	82
Gifts	84

A Word about the Music

The Spinning Top.................................... 87
Scattering Flowers.................................. 87
Rabboni! Master! 89
St. Teresa's Book-mark 90

Young Voices

Sanctuary 92
A Prayer.. 92
To Joseph 93
Stella Matutina...................................... 93
Answer... 94

In Honor of Mary

A Prayer of Praise to Mary 97
The Magnificat 97
Alma Redemptoris 99
Ave Regina.. 99
Regina Coeli.. 99
Salve Regina.. 100
Ave, Maris Stella 101
Salve, Virgo Florens 102
Ave Sanctissima................................... 103
The Canticle of Bernadette 104

The Liturgical Sequences

Dies Irae... 108
Stabat Mater Dolorosa.......................... 110
Victimae Paschali................................. 112
Veni, Sancte Spiritus 113
Lauda Sion.. 114

Psalms and Hymns of Praise

Te Deum Laudamus.............................. 118
De Profundis 120
Adeste Fideles..................................... 121
Jesu, Dulcis Memoria............................ 122
Vexilla Regis 123
Gloria, Laus, et Honor.......................... 123
Pange Lingua Gloriosa.......................... 124
The Reproaches................................... 126

Veni, Creator Spiritus	128
O Salutaris Hostia	130
Tantum Ergo Sacramentum	130
Ave Verum Corpus Natum	131
Adoro Te Devote	132
To the Guardian Angel	132
The Holy Angels	133
Hymn of Thanksgiving	134
Nunc Dimittis	135

From the Olden Times

I Saw Three Ships

This very old ballad has many variations and presents a quaint picture of Our Lady and the good Saint Joseph "on Christmas Day in the morning."

As I sat under a sycamore tree,
A sycamore tree, a sycamore tree,
I looked me out upon the sea
On Christmas Day in the morning.

I saw three ships a-sailing there,
A-sailing there, a-sailing there,
Jesu, Mary and Joseph they bare
On Christmas Day in the morning.

Joseph did whistle and Mary did sing,
Mary did sing, Mary did sing,
And all the bells on earth did ring
For joy Our Lord was born.

O they sailed into Bethlehem!
To Bethlehem, to Bethlehem;
Saint Michael was the steersman,
Saint John sat in the horn.

And all the bells on earth did ring,
On earth did ring, on earth did ring:
"Welcome be Thou, Heaven's King,
On Christmas Day in the morning."

Brown Robin's Confession

Another old ballad that tells of a man who sinned and was saved by Our Lady's intercession.

It fell upon a Wodensday
Brown Robin's men went to sea;
But they saw neither moon nor sun
Nor starlight with their e'e.

"We'll cast lots among us
To see who the man may be."
The lot fell on Brown Robin,
The master man was he.

"It is no wonder," said Brown Robin,
"Although I do not thrive;
For I murdered mine old father," says he;
"I would he were yet alive.

"But tie me to a plank of wood
And throw me in the sea;
And if I sink ye may bid me sink,
If I swim just let me be."

They've tied him to a plank of wood
And thrown him in the sea;
He didna sink though they bade him sink,
He swimmed and they bade let him be.

He hadna been into the sea
An hour but barely three,
Till by and came Our Blessed Ladie,
Her dear young Son her wi'.

"Will ye gang to your men again?
Or will ye gang wi' me?
Will ye gang to the high heavens
Wi' my dear Son and me?"

"I winna gang to my men again,
For they would be feared at me;
But I would gang to the high heavens
Wi' thy dear Son and Thee."

"It's for no honor ye did, Brown Robin,
It's for no good ye did to me;
But it's all for your fair confession
You've made upon the sea."

The Friar of Orders Grey

This old tale in the ballad form does not record what the lady fair said when she received the friar's somewhat startling news. We feel that we should like to know the rest of the story.

It was a Friar of Orders Grey
Walked forth to tell his beads;
And he met with a lady fair
Clad in a pilgrim's weeds.

"Now Christ thee save, thou reverend Friar,
I pray thee tell to me,
If even at yon holy shrine
My true love thou didst see."

"And how should I know your true love
From many another one?"
"O by his cockle hat and staff
And by his sandal shoon."

"O Lady, he is dead and gone;
Lady, he's dead and gone,
And at his head a green grass turf
And at his heels a stone."

Two Old Lenten Rhymes

The first of these old rhymes is an amusing reminder that "fish on Friday" as well as during the Lenten fast has always been a bit of a problem to the housewife. The second, more serious in tone, may well serve as a reminder to those Catholics who in these easy days fail to observe Lent as strictly as they should.

Lenten stuff has come to the town,
The cleansing week comes quickly;
You know well enough you must kneel down;
Come on, take ashes trickly.

Herring, herring, white and red,
Seek out such as be rotten;
Though some be hanged and some be dead
And some be yet forgotten.

Lily-white mussels have no peer;
The fish-wives fetch them quickly,
So he that hath a conscience clear
May stand to his tackle trickly.

Carp is counted very good,
A trim fish and a dainty.
But if it smell once of the mud
Who'll give a groat for twenty?

Then Jack-a-Lent comes jostling in,
With the head piece of a herring,
And saith, "Repent you of your sin,

From the Olden Times

For shame, sirs, leave your swearing."
And to Palm Sunday doth he ride,
With sprats and herrings by his side,
And makes an end of Lenten tide.

. . . .

Now with the slow revolving year,
    Again the Fast we greet.
Which in its mystic circle moves
    Of forty days complete.

That Fast, by Law and Prophet taught,
    By Jesus Christ restored;
Jesus, of seasons and of times
    The Maker and the Lord.

Henceforth more sparing let us be
    Of food, of words, of sleep;
Henceforth beneath a stricter guard
    The roving senses keep;

And let us shun whatever things
    Distract the careless heart;
And let us shut our souls against
    The tyrant tempter's art;

And weep before the Judge and strive
    His vengeance to appease;
Saying to Him with contrite voice
    Upon our bended knees:

Much have we sinned, O Lord, and still
  We sin each day we live;
Yet look in pity from on high,
  And of Thy grace forgive.

The Rune of Hospitality

Organized charity is modern and efficient, but it deprives us of something very precious, the privilege of serving with our own hands God's holy poor. In this poem one cannot help wondering what was the music and what the "listening-place."

I saw a stranger yestereen,
I put food in the eating-place,
Drink in the drinking-place,
Music in the listening-place,
And in the blessed name of the Triune
He blessed myself and my house,
My cattle and my dear ones,
And the lark said in her song,
Often, often, often
Goes the Christ in the stranger's guise.
Often, often, often
Goes the Christ in the stranger's guise.

—*Tr. from the Gaelic by* Thomas Walsh

From the Olden Times

The Rann of the Three

An amusing old Irish explanation of the Holy Trinity.

>Three folds in my garment, yet only one garment I bear;
>Three joints in a finger, yet only one finger is there;
>Three leaves in a shamrock, yet only one shamrock I wear;
>Frost, ice, and snow, these three are nothing but water,
>Three Persons in God, yet only one God is there.

>—*Tr. by* Thomas Walsh

Prayer Before Sleeping

There are several variations of this old English prayer, and most children know at least one of them. Many a person grown to manhood still says some part of the little rhyme even as he did in childhood.

>Matthew, Mark, Luke, and John,
>Bless the bed that I lie on.
>Before I lay me down to sleep,
>I give my soul to Christ to keep.
>Four corners to my bed,
>Four angels overspread,
>Two at foot and two at head,
>Four to carry me when I'm dead.
>I go by sea, I go by land,
>The Lord made me with His right hand.
>If any danger come to me,
>Sweet Jesus Christ, deliver me.

He is the branch and I the flower,
Pray God send me a happy hour,
And if I die before I wake,
I pray that God my soul will take.

The Breastplate of St. Patrick

This is part of an old Gaelic poem. No wonder the Irish people are so strong in faith. St. Patrick taught them well and they remembered.

I arise to-day
Through a mighty strength, the invocation of the Trinity,
Through a belief in the Threeness,
Through confession of the Oneness
Of the Creator of creation.

. . . .

I arise to-day
Through the strength of the love of cherubim,
In obedience of angels,
In service of archangels,
In the hope of resurrection to meet with reward,
In prayers of patriarchs,
In predictions of prophets,
In preachings of apostles,
In faith of confessors,
In innocence of virgins,
In deeds of righteous men.

I arise to-day
Through the strength of heaven;
Light of the sun,
Radiance of the moon,
Splendor of fire,
Speed of lightning,
Swiftness of the wind,
Depth of the sea,
Stability of the earth,
Firmness of the rock.

I arise to-day
Through God's strength to pilot me;
God's might to uphold me,
God's wisdom to guide me,
God's eye to look before me,
God's ear to hear me,
God's word to speak for me,
God's hand to guard me,

God's way to lie before me,
God's shield to protect me,
God's hosts to save me,
From snares of the devil,
From temptations of vices,
From everyone who desires me ill,
Afar or near,
Alone or in a multitude.

Christ with me, Christ before me, Christ behind me,
Christ in me, Christ beneath me, Christ above me,
Christ on my right, Christ on my left,
Christ when I lie down, Christ when I sit down,
Christ when I arise,
Christ in the heart of every man who thinks of me,
Christ in the mouth of every man who speaks of me,
Christ in the eye that sees me,
Christ in the ear that hears me.
I arise to-day
Through a mighty strength, the invocation of the Trinity,
Through a belief in the Threeness,
Through a confession of the Oneness
Of the Creator of Creation.

From the Olden Times

The Irish Te Deum

Resignation to God's will is a special grace and not easily achieved. It will be seen from this bit of verse that the Irish people have it in generous measure.

>Thanks be to God for the light and the darkness;
>Thanks be to God for the hail and the snow;
>Thanks be to God for showers and sunshine;
>Thanks be to God for all things that grow;
>Thanks be to God for lightning and tempest;
>Thanks be to God for weal and for woe;
>Thanks be to God for His own great goodness;
>Thanks be to God that what is, is so;
>Thanks be to God when the harvest is plenty;
>Thanks be to God when the barn is low;
>Thanks be to God when our pockets are empty;
>Thanks be to God when again they o'erflow.
>Thanks be to God that the mass-bell and steeple
>Are heard and are seen throughout Erin's green isle;
>Thanks be to God that the priest and the people
>Are ever united in danger and trial.
>Thanks be to God that the brave sons of Erin
>Have the faith of their fathers as lively as aye;
>Thanks be to God that Erin's fair daughters
>Press close after Mary on heaven's highway.

A Rune of Praise

These ancient Irish prayers are of the very essence of poetry. This one is no exception with its suggestion of a heart overflowing with love for the Master.

      I offer Thee—
Every flower that ever grew,
Every bird that ever flew,
Every wind that ever blew,
    Good God!
Every thunder rolling,
Every church-bell tolling,
Every leaf and sod.

          Laudamus Te!

      I offer Thee—
Every wave that ever moved,
Every heart that ever loved
Thee, Thy Father's well-beloved,
    Dear Lord!
Every river dashing,
Every lightning flashing,
Like an angel's sword.

          Benedicimus Te!

      I offer Thee—
Every cloud that ever swept
O'er the skies, and broke and wept
In rain, and with the flowerets slept,
    My King!

Each communicant praying,
Every angel staying Before Thy throne to
   sing.

Adoremus Te!

   I offer Thee—
Every flake of virgin snow,
Every spring the earth below,
Every human joy and woe,
My love!
O Lord! and all Thy glorious
Self, o'er death victorious,
Throned in Heaven above.

Glorificamus Te!

Take all of them, O darling Lord,
In thy Bless'd Sacrament loved, adored.
Multiply each and every one,
Make each of them into millions–
   Into glorious millions,
   Into gorgeous millions,
Of Glorias, glorious Son! And then,
O dear Lord, listen
Where the tabernacles glisten,
To these praises, Holiest One!

Rhymes and Runes

A Cradle Song

Blue is the traditional color of the Blessed Virgin. Little Bernadette of Lourdes saw her in the Grotto in a "mantle of blue." Many mothers dress their little daughters in blue until they are seven years old in honor of Mary.

> O men from the fields!
>   Come softly within.
> Tread softly, softly,
>   O men coming in!
>
> Mavourneen is going
>   From me and from you,
> Where Mary will fold Him
>   With mantle of blue.
>
> From reek of the smoke
>   And cold of the floor,
> And the peering of things
>   Across the half-door.

O men from the fields!
    Soft, softly come thro'
Mary puts round Him
    Her mantle of blue.

—Padraic Colum

The Christ-Child

The writer of these charming lines is a very famous author, a convert, and an eloquent Catholic apologist. Read his "Lepanto" which tells of one of the crusades. You will not soon forget the stirring refrain, "Don John of Austria is going to the war."

The Christ-Child lay on Mary's lap,
    His hair was like a light.
(O weary, weary were the world,
    But here is all aright!)

The Christ-Child lay on Mary's breast,
    His hair was like a star.
(O stern and cunning are the kings,
    But here the true hearts are.)

. . . .

The Christ-Child stood at Mary's knee,
    His hair was like a crown,
And all the flowers looked up at Him,
    And all the stars looked down.

—Gilbert Keith Chesterton

Our Lord and Our Lady

Another famous and gifted Catholic wrote this poem. He and Chesterton are friends and contemporaries, "both great in body, great in mind, and great in friendship with each other and with God."

> They warned Our Lady for the Child
>   That was Our blessed Lord
> And She took Him into the desert wild,
>   Over the camel's ford.
>
> And a long song She sang to Him
>   And a short story told:
> And She wrapped Him in a woolen cloak
>   To keep Him from the cold.
>
> But when Our Lord was grown a man
>   The Rich they dragged Him down,
> And they crucified Him in Golgotha,
>   Out and beyond the Town.
>
> They crucified Him on Calvary,
>   Upon an April day;
> And because He had been Her little Son
>   She followed Him all the way.
>
> Our Lady stood beside the Cross
>   A little space apart,
> And when She heard Our Lord cry out
>   A sword went through Her Heart.

They laid Our Lord in a marble tomb,
    Dead, in a winding sheet.
But Our Lady stands above the world
    With the White Moon at Her feet.

—Hilaire Belloc

Christmas Morning

A little girl tries to imagine what the stable in Bethlehem really was like. She thinks that Mother Mary's little Boy would look just like her own baby brother. The picture is so real to her that she almost believes that she was actually there and saw the Wise Men coming in after their long journey.

If Bethlehem were here today,
Or this were very long ago,
There wouldn't be a winter time
 Nor any cold or snow.

I'd run out through the garden gate,
And down along the pasture walk;
And off beside the cattle barns
I'd hear a kind of gentle talk.

I'd move the heavy iron chain
And pull away the wooden pin;
I'd push the door a little bit
And tiptoe very softly in.

The pigeons and the yellow hens
And all the cows would stand away;

Their eyes would open wide to see
A lady in the manger hay,

If this were very long ago
And Bethlehem were here today.

And mother held my hand and smiled—
I mean the lady would—and she
Would take the woolly blankets off
Her little Boy so I could see.

His shut-up eyes would be asleep,
And He would look like our John,
And He would be all crumpled too,
And have a pinkish color on.

I'd watch His breath go in and out,
His little clothes would all be white.
I'd slip my finger in His hand
To feel how He could hold it tight.

And she would smile and say, "Take care,"
The mother, Mary, would, "Take care";
And I would kiss His little hand
And touch His hair.

While Mary put the blankets back
The gentle talk would soon begin
And when I'd tiptoe softly out
I'd meet the wise men going in.

—Elizabeth Madox Roberts

Le Coeur de l'Immaculée

Alet, Limoux, France

Mr. Benjamin Musser is a Franciscan Tertiary and a devoted servant of Our Lady to whom he dedicated "A Chaplet of Sanctuaries" from which this poem is taken. It contains fifty poems about various famous shrines of the Blessed Virgin.

Up from Toulouse, September in the air,
Maidens with their white veils; garlands on their hair,
And sober boys are marching, all singing, singing fair,
Salve Regina!

Old men in sabots, going to Alet,
Peaceful old housewives, babies round and gay,
Off to a party on the Queen's birthday,
   Ave Maria!

Honoring her heart, her heart without a stain
(Who dwells in their own hearts, blessed chatelaine),
They pray that her heart through the world will reign,
   O gloriosa Domina!

—Benjamin Francis Musser

The Housewife's Prayer

Many a sorely tried housemother turns to Mary of Nazareth who also knew poverty, worry, and all a housewife's petty cares. It is strange to remember how very young was Mary when God gave the Holy Child into her care. She must have woven His little garments and kept them sweet and clean; she must often have been anxious lest the growing Lad go hungry. The thought of that little household touches the imagination.

Lady, who with tender ward
Didst keep the house of Christ the Lord,
Who didst set forth the bread and wine
Before the Living Wheat and Vine,

Reverently didst make the bed
Whereon was laid the holy Head
That such a cruel pillow prest
For our behoof, on Calvary's crest;
Be beside me while I go
About my labors to and fro.
Speed the wheel and speed the loom,
Guide the needle and the broom,
Make my bread rise sweet and light,
Make my cheese come foamy white;
Yellow may my butter be
As cowslips blowing on the lea.
Homely though my tasks and small,
Be beside me at them all.
Then when I shall stand to face
Jesu in the judgment place,
To me thy gracious help afford,
Who art the Handmaid of the Lord.

—Blanche Mary Kelly

Sheep and Lambs

This lovely poem is easy to learn, and once learned it haunts the memory, especially at the Agnus Dei of the Mass.

All in the April evening,
    April airs were abroad;

The sheep with their little lambs
    Passed me by on the road.

The sheep with their little lambs
    Passed me by on the road;
All in an April evening
    I thought on the Lamb of God.

The lambs were weary and crying
    With a weak, human cry;
I thought on the Lamb of God
    Going meekly to die.

Up in the blue, blue mountains
    Dewy pastures are sweet:
Rest for the little bodies,
    Rest for the little feet.

But for the Lamb of God
    Up on the hill-top green,
Only a cross of shame
    Two stark crosses between.

All in the April evening,
    April airs were abroad;
I saw the sheep with their lambs,
    And thought on the Lamb of God.

—Katherine Tynan Hinkson

A Ballad of Trees and the Master

A mind well stocked with poetry is a great joy to the traveler. In Italy or Spain, the sight of the gray old olive trees brings sharply to mind these beautiful lines.

>Into the woods my Master went,
>Clean forspent, forspent.
>Into the woods my Master came,
>Forspent with love and shame.
>But the olives they were not blind to Him;
>The little gray leaves were kind to Him;
>The thorn-tree had a mind to Him
>When into the woods He came.
>Out of the woods my Master went,
>And He was well content.
>Out of the woods my Master came,
>Content with death and shame.
>When Death and Shame would woo Him last,
>From under the trees they drew Him last:
>'Twas on a tree they slew Him—last
>When out of the woods He came.

—Sidney Lanier

Man of the House

The good St. Joseph, watching and guarding the Holy Child, is always an appealing figure. This poem paints a pleasant picture of the little family at Nazareth at their everyday human tasks. It encourages us to believe that St. Joseph will be quick to help us in our own small daily needs.

Joseph, honored from Sea to Sea,
This is your name that pleases me,
    "Man of the House."

I see you rise at the dawn and light
The fire and blow till the flame is bright.

I see you take the pitcher and carry
The deep well-water for Jesus and Mary.

You knead the corn for the bread so fine,
Gather them grapes from the hanging vine.

There are little feet that are soft and slow,
Follow you whithersoever you go.

There's a little face at your workshop door,
A little One sits down on your floor.

Holds His hands for the shavings curled,
The soft little hands that have made the world.

With Harp and Lute

Mary calls you; the meal is ready;
You swing the Child to your shoulder steady.

I see your quiet smile as you sit
And watch the little Son thrive and eat.

The vine curls by the window space,
The wings of angels cover the face.

Up in the rafters, polished and olden,
There's a dove that broods and his wings are golden.

You who kept them through shine and storm,
A staff, a shelter kindly and warm.

Father of Jesus, husband of Mary,
Hold up your lilies for Sanctuary!

Joseph, honored from Sea to Sea,
Guard me mine and my own roof tree,
    "Man of the House."

—Katherine Tynan Hinkson

The Mother of Judas

After the crucifixion, Mary went with John as her Son had told her to do. She could fall asleep, for after all, although her Son had died, He had died gloriously. But out in the field of the village potter, bought from him for the thirty pieces of silver, lay Judas, a suicide, first to be buried there. His mother could not sleep; she asked the age-old questions that all mothers ask when their sons bring sorrow upon them. To this day in nearly every cemetery is found a "Potter's Field," a burial place for the poor and the stranger.

> Mary, in the house of John,
>   Spent with sorrow, fell asleep;
> But in the lonely potter's field
>   I heard a woman weep.
> "Leading your baby feet, my son,
>   What turning did I take amiss?
> What did I do or leave undone
>   That you should come to this?"
> All night she made above her dead
>   That comfortless and bitter cry,
> "What did I say or leave unsaid
>   That thus my child should die?"

—Amelia Josephine Burr

St. Peter

Nearly all of us have favorite saints, but few feel on such friendly terms with St. Peter. We hear Mass with awe at his tomb in St. Peter Vatican and find it easier to think of him as Peter, the Rock, the head of the Church, than as Peter the simple fisherman, who betrayed his Lord when the cock crew and afterwards wept so bitterly. The play, "The Upper Room," by Robert Hugh Benson, gives a good picture of St. Peter.

> Each has his saint, and one may dream
> Of Francis walking in a field,
> Another turn where Michael dark
> Springs slim and wild to lift his shield.
>
> A third may let his loving light
> Upon the whirling torch of Paul;
> I dream of Peter's shaggy head
> Bent blinking o'er his haul.
>
> I smile for that old simple tongue,
> So quick, so breathless to begin,
> That snubbed and silenced o'er and o'er
> Could never lock its wonder in.
>
> I kneel to those old dogged feet
> That padded on from shore to city,
> I cry for that old troubled heart
> That tried to tempt God out of pity.
>
> And what of that old broken soul
> That crept out sobbing from the light
> Closing its ears against the bird
> And beating blindly through the night!

How could he know except in tales
The majesty, the rune of law,
An old man bred to nets and sails,
Betrayed by ignorance and awe?

Ah, dear to me! Ah, dear to me!
That fear, that flying from the rod,
That ancient infidelity
Rewarded by a risen God.

—Eileen Duggan

Ash Wednesday

As we light our candle or votive light and whisper to God or His Saints our own hopes or fears or thanksgivings, we often wonder what happy heart or burdened soul set the other lights aglow. Do you ever light your candle from another and pray for that other intention?

Of votive lights there were only seven,
And each burned a prayer to the God in heaven.
Five candles were blue, one green, and one red,
Six burned for the living, and one for the dead.
The belfry was old and the church was bare,
Only the voice of the wind and the rain was there.
"I can snuff the candles," said the voice of the rain
As downward it drifted through a cracked window
    pane,
"I can snuff the candles!" said the wind in the eaves,
"Who cares for a hope, or a heart that grieves?"

And the blue lights flickered, and the green one died
Before the bowed head of the meek Crucified.
But the last to flicker was the one bright red—
The candle that burned for the lonely dead.

—Rosa Zagnoni Marinoni

The Good Joan

During the World War, French soldiers believed that Jeanne d'Arc, the heroic maid, rode once more to battle to save her France. She is Saint Joan now, having been canonized not very long ago.

>Along the thousand roads of France,
>Now there, now here, swift as a glance,
>A cloud, a mist blown down the sky,
>*Good Joan of Arc goes riding by.*

In Domremy at candlelight,
The orchards blowing rose and white
About the shadowy houses lie;
And Joan of Arc goes riding by.

On Avignon there falls a hush,
Brief as the singing of a thrush
Across old gardens April-high;
And Joan of Arc goes riding by.

The women bring the apples in,
Round Arles when the long gusts begin,
Then sit them down to sob and cry;
And Joan of Arc goes riding by.

Dim fall the hoofs down old Calais;
In Tours a flash of silver-gray,
Like flaw of rain in a clear sky;
And Joan of Arc goes riding by.

Who saith that ancient France shall fail,
A rotting leaf driv'n down the gale?
Then her sons know not how to die;
Then good God dwells no more on high!

Tours, Arles, and Domremy reply!
For Joan of Arc goes riding by.

—Lizette Woodworth Reese

Contrition Across the Waves
(Father Damien of Molokai, 1840-1888)

It is an unforgettable picture that this poem paints for us—the good priest, Father Damien, the "Apostle of the Lepers," cut off from even the spiritual consolations of the Church, seeking a confessor on any chance boat, humbly confessing his sins from the open sea, while onlookers thrilled at the beauty of his sacrifice.

> Damien lived with lepers;
> > Damien lived for them
> On a margin of the world
> > That touched not any hem.
>
> Damien was a priest of God
> > Whose Church held all his law;
> So, every year, he rowed alone
> > Until some ship he saw.
>
> Though often disappointed,
> > Anxious and so tired,
> His sacramental search went on
> > By faithful love inspired.
>
> "A priest on board?" would Damien call;
> > If one came to the rail,
> Damien confessed his sins
> > While a man stood, listening, pale.

On a margin of the world
    That touched not any hem,
Damien lived with lepers;
    Damien died for them.

—Caroline Giltinan

In Brittany

Not only in Brittany, but everywhere in this wide world the door of the Catholic Church stands open and white tapers carry the prayers of the faithful up to God.

In Brittany the churches
    All day are open wide,
That anyone who wishes to
    May pray or rest inside.
The priests have rusty cassocks,
    The priests have shaven chins,
And poor old bodies go to them
    With lists of little sins.

In Brittany the churches
    Are cool and white and quaint,
With here and there a crucifix
    And here and there a saint;
And here and there a little shrine,
    With candles short or tall
That Bretons light for love of Him
    The Lord who loveth all.

—E.V. Lucas

Spiritism

Here is an unusual but potent reason why we should never be guilty of the discourtesy to God of consulting fortune-tellers, crystal-gazers, and others who offer a "keyhole" view of the unknown.

This pathway marked No Thoroughfare
Is obviously barred,
But vulgar people love to stare
In someone else's yard.

It is not reverent but rude
To spy beyond the bounds
Like raw plebeians who intrude
Upon patrician grounds

And bribe the servants to undo
The door a little crack—
A burglar's glimpse, a keyhole view,
Behind the master's back.

A scandal, so it seems to me,
The way they force the doors
To trespass on the privacy
Of their superiors.

How much more fitting to await
The summons to attend,
Ride proudly through the open gate
And enter as a friend.

—Robert Hillyer

The Ballad of Father Gilligan

The lot of the country priest with a big scattered parish is a hard one. One cannot read this poem without feeling a throb of relief with the good old priest when he finds how God has had compassion on his weariness.

> The old priest Peter Gilligan
> Was weary night and day;
> For half his flock were in their beds,
> Or under green sods lay.
>
> Once while he nodded on a chair,
> At the moth-hour of eve,
> Another poor man sent for him,
> And he began to grieve.
>
> "I have no rest, nor joy, nor peace,
> For people die and die";
> And after cried he, "God forgive!
> My body spake, not I."
>
> He knelt and leaning on the chair
> He prayed and fell asleep;
> And the moth-hour went from the fields,
> And stars began to peep.
>
> Then slowly into millions grew,
> And leaves shook in the wind;
> And God covered the world with shade,
> And whispered to mankind.

Upon the time of sparrow chirp
When the moths came once more,
The old priest Peter Gilligan
Stood upright on the floor.

"Mavrone, Mavrone! The man has died,
While I slept on the chair";
He roused his horse out of its sleep,
And rode with little care.

He rode now as he never rode,
By rocky lane and fen;
The sick man's wife opened the door;
"Father! You come again!"

"And is the poor man dead?" he cried.
"He died an hour ago."
The old priest Peter Gilligan
In grief swayed to and fro.

"When you were gone, he turned and died
As merry as a bird."
The old priest Peter Gilligan
He knelt him at that word.

"He Who hath made the night of stars
For souls, who tire and bleed,
Sent one of His great angels down
To help me in my need.

"He Who is wrapped in purple robes,
With planets in His care

Had pity on the least of things
Asleep upon a chair."

—William Butler Yeats

The Friar

The cheerful Franciscan friars, on foot or on mule-back, begging their way in holy poverty even as their saintly founder taught them, are a familiar sight in the old country. It is a difficult life, but a happy one. Coarse wool to wear and old scraps to eat seem a meager lot indeed, but it would be hard to find a discontented Franciscan.

Barefooted, in his hood and cloak of brown,
    Mounted upon his burro's chubby back
    To beg the pious alms that fill his sack
The old Franciscan starts at dawn for town.
Behind him sounds the early belfry down
    To call to Mass the faithful in his track;
    The summons floats afar into the wrack
Of pink and golden clouds, the dawning's crown.
His breviary at his elbow tucked away,
His rosary rattling heavily with his sway,
    He reckons that his givers shall not lag;
And hearkens as he paces down the road.
    Between the burro's braying for the load,
    The wind that whistles through his empty bag.

—Tr. from the Spanish of Julian del Casal by Thomas Walsh

Grace for Light

Among the many charming old Irish customs, that here described is one of the most delightful. It may probably be traced to one of the ceremonies of Holy Saturday, the blessing of the new fire.

When we were little childen we had a quare wee house,
    Away up in the heather by the head o' Brabla' Bum;
The hares we'd see them scootin', an' we'd hear the crowin' grouse,
    An' when we'd all be in at night ye'd not get room to turn.

The youngest two She'd put to bed, their faces to the wall,
    An' the lave of us could sit aroun', just anywhere we might;
Herself 'ud take the rush-dip an' light it for us all,
    An' *"God be thanked!"* she would say,—*"now we have a light."*

Then we be to quet the laughin' an' pushin' on the floor,
    An' think on One who called us to come and be forgiven;
Himself 'ud put his pipe down, an' say the good word more,
    "May the Lamb o' God lead us all to the Light o' Heaven!"

There's a wheen things that used to be an' now has had
   their day,
   The nine Glens of Antrim can show ye many a
      sight;
But not the quare wee house where we lived up Brabla'
   way,
   Nor a child in all the nine Glens that knows the
      grace for light.

—Moira O'Neill

Mary Shepherdess

To the old, the poor, the homeless, the sinner, Mary is the shepherdess who calls home their weary souls.

When the heron's in the high wood and the last long
   furrow's sown,
With the herded cloud before her and her sea-sweet
   raiment blown,
Comes Mary, Mary Shepherdess, a-seeking for her
   own.

Saint James he calls the righteous folk, Saint John he
   calls the kind,

Saint Peter calls the valiant men all to loose or bind,
But Mary seeks the little souls that are so hard to find.

All the little sighing souls born of dust's despair,
They who fed on bitter bread when the world was
   bare,—
Frighted of the glory gates and the starry stair.

All about the windy down, housing in the ling,
Underneath the alder-bough, linnet-light they cling,
Frighted of the shining house where the martyrs sing.

Crying in the ivy bloom, fingering at the pane,
Grieving in the hollow dark, lone along the rain,—
Mary, Mary Shepherdess, gather them again.

And O, the wandering women know, in workhouse
   and in shed,
They dream on Mary Shepherdess with doves about
   her head,
And pleasant posies in her hand, and sorrow
   comforted.

Sighing: There's my little lass, faring fine and free,
    There's the little lad I laid by the holly tree,
Dreaming: There's my nameless bairn laughing at her
    knee.

When the bracken harvest's gathered and frost is on
    the loam,
When the dream goes out in silence and the ebb runs
    out in foam,
Mary, Mary Shepherdess, she bids the lost lambs home.

If I had a little maid to turn my tears away,
If I had a little lad to lead me when I'm gray
All to Mary Shepherdess they'd fold their hands and
    pray.

—Marjorie L. C. Pickthall

Ambition

The Kilmers are a much-loved family. When Joyce Kilmer went to France with the "Fighting 69th" in the World War and was killed in action there, thousands mourned with his gifted wife, Aline, and their interesting children.

Kenton and Deborah, Michael and Rose,
These are fine children as all the world knows;
But into my arms in my dreams every night
Come Peter and Christopher, Faith and Delight.

Kenton is tropical, Rose is pure white,
Deborah shines like a star in the night;

Michael's round eyes are as blue as the sea,
And nothing on earth could be dearer to me.

But where is the baby with Faith can compare?
What is the color of Peterkin's hair?
Who can make Christopher clear to my sight,
Or show me the eyes of my daughter Delight?

When people inquire I always just state:
"I have four nice children and hope to have eight.
Though the first four are pretty and certain to please,
Who knows but the rest may be nicer than these?"

—Aline Kilmer

Multiplication

One of the happy things for the Catholic traveler is that wherever he goes he is sure of friends. One of the first things he looks for is a church, and there he finds the familiar faces of Christ and His Mother and all the friendly saints. God's house is always home to a Catholic.

I take my leave with sorrow of Him I love so well;
I look my last upon His small and radiant prison cell;
O happy lamp! to serve Him with never ceasing light!
O happy flame! to tremble forever in His sight!

I leave the holy quiet for the loudly human train,
And my heart that He has breathed upon is filled with
    lonely pain.
O King, O Friend, O Lover! What sorer grief can be
In all the reddest depths of Hell than banishment from
    Thee?

But from my window as I speed across the sleeping
    land
I see the towns and villages wherein His houses stand.
Above the roofs I see a cross outlined against the night,
And I know that there my Lover dwells in His sacra-
    mental might.

Dominions kneel before Him, and Powers kiss His feet
Yet for me He keeps His weary watch in the turmoil of
    the street;
The King of Kings awaits me, wherever I may go,
O who am I that He should deign to love and serve me
    so?

—Joyce Kilmer

Kings

"Christmas in the trenches!" Many a soldier knee-deep in mud, blind instrument of man's greed and cruelty, must have thought such thoughts as these on Christmas morning.

> The kings of the earth are men of might,
> And cities are burned for their delight,

And the skies rain death in the silent night,
   And the hills belch death all day!

But the King of Heaven, Who made them all,
Is fair and gentle and very small;
He lies in the straw, by the oxen's stall—
   Let them think of Him to-day!

—Joyce Kilmer

Little Serenade

Kenton, the eldest son of the Kilmer family, now a young man, has followed the family tradition and is himself a poet. He attended school at St. Mary's College in Kansas, at Georgetown University, and has been doing post-graduate work in philosophy at the Catholic University in Washington.

You will be enough for me
   My whole life long;
Fire my heart and guide my art
   And fill my song.

Lithe my hand at your command
   And quick and strong.
Take me for your servitor
   My whole life long.

—*Kenton Kilmer*

To the Lighted Lady Window

Wherever we see an image of Christ Himself, of His most holy Mother, or even of our favorite saints, a warm feeling of friendliness possesses us, and we feel impelled to speak a word of greeting as we are passing by.

I kiss my hand to you,
    Mary, Holy Mother!
I kiss my hand to you,
    Jesus, little brother!

Lady, I love your robe
    Like a wave in a deep sea;
Your aureole of stars
    Is very dear to me;

And the beauty of the soul
    That met the Holy Ghost,
And the wonder of the life
    Wherein the guest was Host.
But Lady, even more,—
    And you would have it said,—
I love the little Child
    That shines above your head.

I kiss my hand again,
    Mary, Holy Mother;
I kiss my hand again,
    Jesus, little Brother.

—Marguerite Wilkinson

From Convent Cell and Cloister

WITH HARP AND LUTE

The Altar Boy

The poems of that gifted Jesuit, Father Feeney, suggest to us many ideas. He makes us see what a wonderful privilege is that of the boy who serves God at the altar; how the good Saint Joseph, a carpenter himself, was sad because he could not mend the wretched stable, and how later he watched over the Holy Child, picking up the nails on the floor lest they bruise the tender little feet. He makes us remember how sweet and frail and young was God's holy Mother, and helps us to realize why so many people find happiness in following the meek Jesus on His way to Calvary.

His cheeks grow red from the candle heat
As the carpet under his noiseless feet.

And no two stars could be half so bright
As his deep brown eyes in the candle-light.

An angel he seems with his surplice wings,
Who knows when God is to come, and rings.

And the clouds from the censer swinging there
A fragrance leave in his golden hair.

It fills us all with a wondrous dread,
His nearness unto the Holy Bread.

Now I wonder what path in life he'll plan:
A doctor—a lawyer—a merchantman?

God keep him always there we pray,
Treading the altar's plush highway.
—Leonard Feeney, S. J.

The Lonely Crib

I pity the slender Mother-maid
    For the night was dark and her heart afraid
As she knelt in the straw where the beasts had trod
    And crooned and cooed to the living God.

And I pity Saint Joseph whose heart wept o'er The
    ruined stall and the broken floor
And the roof unmended for Him and her,—
    And to think himself was a carpenter!

O Thrones, Dominions, spirits of power,
    Where were you there in that bitter hour!
And where the Cherubim-wings withal
    To cover the wind-holes in the wall!

Three lambs a shepherd-boy brought, and these
    Were Powers and Principalities;
And Ariel, Uriel, angels bright,
    Were two frail rays from a lantern-light.

The faded eyes of a wondering ass
>   Were dreamy mirrors where visions pass.
And a poor old ox in the stable dim,
>   His moo was the song of the Seraphim!

—Leonard Feeney, S. J.

The Welcome

No music He heard, and no angels He saw
>   As He lay in His wrappings of linen and straw;
And the ox and the ass could not kneel and adore
>   For the poor creatures never were angels before.

The palace He found was an old cattle stall
>   With a broken-down roof and a windowless wall,
And it looked so ashamed of its spider-worn wood;
>   But it tried to be Heaven, as well as it could.

A dull stable-lantern that hung dark and dim
>   Was the small bit of moonlight that flickered on Him.
Now it longed to be beautiful, starry and bright,
>   And it sputtered and wept for the dearth of its light.

But a Lady of Beauty stood over His head
>   While she gathered the strewings about for His bed.
And her soul was as sweet as a fresh-budding rose
>   And as white as the fusion of myriad snows.

And her hands did not soil this immaculate prize,
>   And her breath did not sully the bloom in His eyes.

On her breast sweet and safe could He slumber and nod:
The lily-white village-maid, Mother of God.

—Leonard Feeney, S. J.

Nails

Whenever the bright blue nails would drop
Down on the floor of his carpenter shop,
Saint Joseph, prince of carpenter men,
Would stoop to gather them up again;
For he feared for two little sandals sweet,
And very easy to pierce they were
As they pattered over the lumber there
And rode on two little sacred feet.
But alas, on a hill between earth and heaven
One day—two nails in a cross were driven,
And fastened it firm to the sacred feet
Where once rode two little sandals sweet;
And Christ and His mother looked off in death
Afar—to the valley of Nazareth,
Where the carpenter's shop was spread with dust
And the little blue nails, all packed in rust,
Slept in a box on the window-sill;
And Joseph lay sleeping under the hill.

—Leonard Feeney, S. J.

With Harp and Lute

A Gift of Flowers

A basket of roses for the Royal House of David—
    A harvest of blossoms in the Spring.
Chrysanthemums and daisies for the ladies of
    Jerusalem
    And lilies for the daughters of the King.

Lilies out in Galilee, opening in April,—
    Sunflowers to pluck and carry home;
Poppies for high priestesses and myriads of tulips
    For the wives of the Emperors of Rome.

But ah, come and wander, meek Maid of Nazareth,
    Wander by the brook and by the lea;
A sweet, little, meek, frail, lonely-by-the-wayside,
    Shadow-blue violet for thee!

—Leonard Feeney, S. J.

The Way of the Cross

Along the dark aisles
    Of a chapel dim,
The little lame girl
    Drags her withered limb.

And all alone she searches
    The shadows on the walls
To find the three pictures
    Where Jesus falls.

—Leonard Feeney, S. J.

From Convent Cell and Cloister

Ad Matrem in Caelis

Father O'Donnell, now deceased, was the beloved president of Notre Dame University and a friend of Knute Rockne, the hero of every boy. He gives us a pleasant picture of his mother who loved flowers, walking in the heavenly gardens with those gentlest of saints, St. Francis and the Little Flower.

I can remember flowers at your hand,
    Summer and autumn, spring,
Nor less when winter in our northern land
    Forbade your bird to sing,—
    Geraniums in the dining room
    For you would bloom.

Dear heart, in gardens of the ever fair
    Sweet summer of the saints
I know you walk, unchanged, in a gentle air
    Where the breath of roses faints,
    And no eyes are happier than your eyes
    In Paradise.

And if beside you walk two saints of God,
    I know what saints they are,
Lover of birds and bees and bloom, who trod
    Umbria, afar,
    And the sweetest bird of time's last hour,—
    The Little Flower.

—Charles L. O'Donnell, S. S. C.

Johneen

Father Carroll, the editor of Ave Maria, paints a pleasant picture of an old-fashioned Irish-Catholic family. From families like these came priests and nuns to serve God in far places.

There's ten of ye now, and twenty long years in between
From Maurice, the man of the house, to little Johneen
But I wouldn't spare one, not for all the rich pearls of a queen.
        Ah, my heart craves ye all!
For ye light up the gloom of the place,
As Our Lord lit the dark of the cave by the light of His face.

Yes, ten of ye all, and Maurice as tall as a pine;
Then Mary come Candlemas day will be finishing nine;
And Johneen—O come lay your little heart here
   against mine!
      Yes, 'tis I loves ye all:
Maurice and Mike and Kathleen,
And, pulse of my heart, yourself, little Johneen.
When the house does be empty the long, lonesome
   stretch of the day,
With only Johneen in the cradle a-sleeping away,
The tears do come down from my eyes and I trying to
   pray!
      O, I dream of ye all,
And the crosses God sends, and our needs—
Sweet Savior, forgive me!—ye come between me and
   the beads.

But, thank God, sure ye're hearty and brimful of inno-
   cent joys,
And of nights round the kitchen ye fill up the house
   with your noise.
Virgin pure, keep ye innocent always, my girls and my
   boys!
      For I've mothered ye all
Down those twenty long years in between
From Maurice, who stoops at the door, to little
   Johneen.

                —Patrick J. Carroll, C. S. C.

With Harp and Lute

October of the Angels

October is commonly celebrated as the month of angels, and many people say the Litany of the Holy Angels every day. It is a good time to pay our small meed of reverence to these unseen friends—to Gabriel, Raphael, and the valiant Michael, as well as to our too little appreciated guardian angels.

>I hear the angels marching
>>Adown the windless air:
>
>Not a foot-fall! Not a wind-rush!
>>Yet I hear them passing there.
>
>Behind a screen of silence
>>Their golden trumpets blow
>
>As down the air's broad avenues
>>Their rattling squadrons go.
>
>The hills and woods and meadows
>>Like crowds at state parades,
>
>Are hushed while God's strong grenadiers
>>File down aerial glades.
>
>The world is hung with pennons
>>And filmy snares are spun
>
>From every standing thing to catch
>>The colors in the sun.
>
>And every summer rainbow
>>Has been rifled to array

The forests and the valleys
    To make a brave display.

The elms are clad in yellows,
    The oaks in scarlet bold,
The sumacs in vermilion,
    The fields in russet gold.

Late morning-glories bugle
    Blasts of color to the sky
And the winds forget their errands when
    God's troops go marching by.

                  —James J. Daly, S. J.

Canticle of the Sun

One of the truly great poets of the church is the humble "Poverello," St. Francis of Assisi. One day after a forty nights' vigil he had an ecstasy, upon which he asked Brother Leo to write for him. Then he intoned the "Canticle of the Sun." It was written down verbatim by Brother Leo, who was called "il Pecorello" or "little Sheep of God," and Brother Pacifico helped to fit the words to the rhythm. St. Francis wanted a band of "singing friars" to preach the gospel of poverty and happiness. Little did he dream that we today would delight to read of Brother Sun and Sister Moon and all the creatures in his canticle.

    Most High Omnipotent, good Lord, to Thee
    The praises and the honor and the glory be!
    All blessings, O most High, befit Thee only,
    And no man is worthy to speak of Thee!

Be praised, O My Lord, by all Thy creatures!
And chiefly by Monsignor Brother Sun,
Whom in the day Thou lightenest for us;
For fair is he and radiant with resplendence;
And of Thee, Most High, beareth he the semblance.

Be praised by Sister Moon and Stars of Night:
In Heaven Thou hast made them, precious, fair and
    bright.
Be praised, O My Lord, by Brother Wind,
By Air and Cloud and Sky and every Clime,
By whom Thou givest sustenance unto all kind!

By Sister Water, O My Lord, be praised!
Useful is she and lowly, precious and chaste.

Be praised, O My Lord, by Brother Fire,
By whom Thou lightenest our steps at night,
And fair is he and merry, masterful and of might!

Be praised, O My Lord, by our Mother, Sister Earth,
Who governeth and sustaineth us and giveth birth
To divers fruits and colored flowers and to herbs!

O bless and praise my Lord and thankful be
And serve My Lord with great humility!

Be praised, My Lord, by my Sister Death, our death of
    the body,
From whom no man living can flee;
Woe is for them who die in mortal sin.

But blessed are those found in Thy most holy Will,
For to them the second death can work no ill.

—St. Francis of Assisi

Hymn of Love

So many boys bear the name of the great Saint Francis Xavier, the Apostle of Japan, that the very initials F. X. connote a Catholic boy. These words, the confession of his love of the Divine Master, appear in many prayer books.

> O God, Thou art the object of my love,
> Not for the hope of endless joys above,
> Nor for the fear of endless pains below
> Which those who love Thee not must undergo.
> For me, and such as me, Thou once didst bear
> The ignominious cross, the nails, the spear;
> A thorny crown transpierced Thy sacred brow;
> What bloody sweats from every member flow!
> Such as then was and is Thy love for me,
> Such is and shall be still my love for Thee;
> Thy love, O Jesus, will I ever sing—
> O God of love, sweet Saviour, dearest King.
>
> —St. Francis Xavier

To-day

Father Faber, educated at famous English colleges, followed Cardinal Newman into the Church. Many of his hymns are known to Catholics the world over.

>Lord, for to-morrow and its needs
>   I do not pray;
>Keep me, my God, from stain of sin
>   Just for to-day.
>Let me both diligently work
>   And duly pray;
>Let me be kind in word and deed
>   Just for to-day,
>Let me be slow to do my will,
>   Prompt to obey;
>Help me to mortify my flesh,
>   Just for to-day.
>Let me no wrong or idle word,
>   Unthinking, say;
>Set Thou a seal upon my lips,
>   Just for to-day.
>Let me in season, Lord, be grave,
>   In season, gay;
>Let me be faithful to Thy grace
>   Just for to-day.
>And if to-day my tide of life
>   Should ebb away,
>Give me Thy sacraments divine,
>   Sweet Lord, to-day.

In purgatory's cleansing fires
    Brief be my stay;
O bid me, if to-day I die,
    Go home to-day.
So for to-morrow and its needs,
    I do not pray;
But keep me, guide me, love me, Lord,
    Just for to-day.

—Frederick William Faber

O Jesu

Father Olier, the founder of the famous Sulpician order, was a brilliant young graduate of the Sorbonne, who devoted himself to God after a miraculous restoration of his failing eyesight. He labored with St. Vincent de Paul among the poor of Paris before going to the Church of St. Sulpice, where he established a seminary. There are several Sulpician seminaries in this country.

O Jesus, living in Mary,
Come and live in Thy servants,
In the spirit of Thy holiness,
In the fulness of Thy might,
In the truth of Thy virtues,
In the perfection of Thy ways,
In the communion of Thy mysteries.
Subdue every hostile power.
    In Thy spirit,
        For the glory of Thy Father,
            Amen.

—Jean Jacques Olier

Prayer for a Priest

Our priests urge us earnestly to pray for them because they need our prayers so much, but we often forget. This poem may remind us of their needs.

> Give him, Lord, eyes to behold the truth,
> A seeing sense that knows the eternal right,
> A heart with pity filled and gentlest ruth,
> A manly faith that makes all darkness light,
> Give him the power to labor for mankind,
> Make him the mouth of such as cannot speak;
> Eyes let him be to groping men and blind;
> A conscience to the base; and to the weak
> Let him be hands and feet, and to the foolish mind;
> And lead still further on such as Thy Kingdom seek.

WITH HARP AND LUTE

Veni, Domine Jesu!

Father Rawes was another Anglican like Father Faber, who became a Catholic. He joined the Oblates of St. Charles at Bayswater and became Superior of that congregation.

O Jesus, hidden God, I cry to Thee;
O Jesus, hidden Light, I turn to Thee;
O Jesus, hidden Love, I run to Thee;
With all the strength I have I worship Thee;
With all the love I have I cling to Thee;
With all my soul I long to be with Thee,
And fear no more to fail, or fall from Thee.

O Jesus, deathless Love, Who seekest me,
Thou Who didst die for longing love of me,
Thou King, in all Thy beauty, come to me,
White-robed, blood-sprinkled, Jesus, come to me.
And go no more, dear Lord, away from me.

O sweetest Jesus, bring me home to Thee;
Free me, O dearest Lord, from all but Thee,
And all the chains that keep me back from Thee;
Call me, O thrilling Love, I follow Thee;
Thou art my all, and I love naught but Thee.

O hidden Love, Who now art loving me;
O wounded Love, Who once wast dead for me;
O patient Love, Who weariest not of me—
O bear with me till I am lost in Thee;
O bear with me till I am found in Thee.

—HENRY AUGUSTUS RAWES

Anima Christi

The great Saint Ignatius Loyola was a Spaniard of noble birth. He was a soldier when called to take up the arms of the spirit and fight for the glory of God. Recovering from a broken leg, he read the life of Christ by a Saxon monk and the lives of the saints and determined to imitate them. The result was the illustrious society of Jesuits whose colleges and universities now circle the earth.

Soul of Christ, be my sanctification;
Body of Christ, be my salvation;
Blood of Christ, fill all my veins;
Water from Christ's side, wash out my stains;
Passion of Christ, my comfort be,
O good Jesu, listen to me.
In Thy wounds I fain would hide,
Ne'er to be parted from Thy side.
Guard me when the foes assail me;
Guide me when my feet shall fail me;
Bid me come to Thee above,
With the saints to sing Thy love,
Forever and ever,
Amen.

—St. Ignatius Loyola

Petitions of Saint Augustine

Saint Augustine, son of a Christian mother, the good Saint Monica, and a pagan father, was baptized by Saint Ambrose and became first a priest and then a bishop. A renowned scholar, his "Confessions" is one of the world's classics.

> O Lord Jesus, let me know myself, let me know Thee,
> And desire nothing else but Thee.
> Let me hate myself and love Thee,
> And do all things for sake of Thee.
> Let me humble myself and exalt Thee,
> And think of nothing else but Thee,
> Let me die to myself and live in Thee,
> And take whatever happens as from Thee.
> Let me forsake myself and walk after Thee,
> And ever desire to follow Thee.
>
> Let me flee myself and turn to Thee,
> That so I may be defended by Thee.
> Let me fear for myself, let me fear Thee,
> And be among those who are chosen by Thee,
> Let me distrust myself and trust in Thee,
> And ever obey for the love of Thee.
> Let me cleave to nothing but only to Thee,
> And ever be poor for sake of Thee.
> Look upon me that I may love Thee;
> Call me that I may see Thee,
> And forever possess Thee.
> Amen.

Christmas in Provence

Sister Madeleva of the Congregation of the Holy Cross is one of the most brilliant of our teaching nuns. Some of her essays are widely used in secular colleges, and she is regarded as an authority in many lines of research. She holds several degrees, has done graduate work at Oxford University, and is a living refutation of the fairly common idea that nuns are just pious persons who rather like to pray.

I

The Serenade

This age-old church, dream-stricken yesterday,
Has wakened into loveliness and light,
And all Provence is in its arms tonight,
And all its tambourines and fifes are gay.
The dull, encumbering ages fall away;
Templar and king kneel in the ancient rite

With torches' blaze and candles tall and white
And a Child cradled on the fresh-strewn hay.

Then the night fills with song, laughing and
    leaping,
This music of a thousand lyric years,
A serenade of love where love lies sleeping,
The minstrelsy of God where God appears,
And where I kneel, bemused, song-shaken,
    weeping,
A happy-hearted troubadour in tears.

II

Midnight Mass

Tonight this city seated on a hill
Wears its mediaeval fortress like a crown
Above a brow too peace-possessed to frown.
Its ancient church watches the darkness fill
With quiet aureoles of light that spill
Through little streets that clamber up the town.
Here ancient, royal kings have lain them down,
And here, this night, a King will rest Him still.

I had not known that night could be so holy;
I had not thought that peace could be so deep.
O passion of night and peace, possess me solely!
O passion of love, be mine this night to keep!

From Convent Cell and Cloister

O little, climbing streets, lead me up slowly
To where the King I wait for lies asleep!
— Sister M. Madeleva, C. S. C.

The Sheep Herd

A Benedictine nun tells us what was in the mind of one of the simple shepherds who went to Bethlehem and saw a new-born Baby in His young mother's arms with a great star overhead.

I am a shepherd—I have hated
The smell of damp sheep in the rain—
The pain
Of clouted shoes on weary feet,
The silly barking of watch-dogs in the night—
The blinding light
Of summer suns on hillsides without shade.
Nor anything I did not wish was not,
From hoar-frost on the meadow grass
To dizzy stars that blinked on stupidly and
    bright.
Last night

I went with other men who tended sheep
Over to Bethlehem to see—
We did not know just what we'd come to see
Who'd followed up a cloud of singing wings.
Until we came to where a young girl held
A little Baby on her lap and smiled.

She made me think of flowers.
White flowers on long stems and blue night
    skies.
Nothing happened—
But today
I have been shaken with the joy
Of seeing hoar-frost wings
Atilt upon tall grasses! The sun
Upon the sheep—making their gray backs white
And silvery
Has hurt me with its beauty, and I heard
The echoes of the barking watch-dogs break
Like silver bells against the quiet hills.

—Sister Mariella, O. S. B.

The Knight

Sister Maryanna, a Dominican nun, compares the missioners of today with the knights of olden times.

He rides no dashing charger in the tournament of life;
    No snowy plume waves o'er his helmet's crest;

His shield is moral courage midst the din of daily
> strife.
> He sings, as forth he fares upon his quest.
At dawn he seeks the Holy Grail, where waxen tapers
> shine,
> In dim-lit chancel, at a Royal Board,
Nor asks he sweeter guerdon at this ever-hallowed
> shrine
> Than to commune, in silence, with his Lord.

He clasps his lady's token now—a silver chain of beads,
> Then forth again, to jousts where lances ring.
His strength is turned to valiant acts, his hands to
> noble deeds,
> His eyes are ever fixed on Christ, his King.

—Sister Maryanna, O. P.

Mother

Few things in life give so much satisfaction as gifts to enhance the beauty of the altar in God's temple. Some give money to buy rich vestments and golden vessels, others set fine stitches in exquisite laces or linens, while still others have only a few fresh flowers to offer, but the last may well be best, for the more personal the service the greater the joy in serving.

I often picture you among the flowers;
Sweet peas you loved the best and tended hours

In afternoon suns, when, for Love's dear sake,
"Fresh garlands for the altar," you would make

And press them to your lips ... a message told
For absent ones ... and you were growing old ...

You watched until some neighbor's boy would pass;
To him you gave your gift for morning Mass.

And when I see these flowers now, your eyes,
Lovely blue, smile at me from Paradise.

Dear heart, I see you waiting in the grass
With fresh bouquets for early morning Mass!

—Sister M. Eulalia, R. S. M.

A Question of Sacrifice

(For Margaret)

Sister Eulalia, a member of the Religious of Sisters of Mercy of the Union, who wrote the last poem, wrote this one for her sister who too wished to be a nun, but gave up her own will to stay at home and care for "Mother." She was often the messenger who took the flowers to early Mass.

A light comes in your face, a sudden glow,
And in your yearning eyes, a dream takes fire,
Caught from the embers of your youth's desire:
To take the highway for the King, to know
The world's far end, and farther end to go
To seek the lambs and sheep among the brier,
And rescue unloved infants from the mire,
Or, pray in cloister, if He willed it so.
You were not destined to reclaim the young,

Or help in pastures where the lambs are fed,
Or keep the watch while matin psalms are sung,
Or comfort hearts whose sighs are for the dead.
You gave your life to her who gave you birth,
Your hands held out her last white peace on earth.

—Sister M. Eulalia, R. S. M.

The Vocation of St. Francis

If the young Francis, still far removed from sainthood, could school himself to touch the leper; if Father Damien and many unknown priests and nuns could give their lives to them, perhaps we could all accept a little more pleasantly the disagreeable things in life. Generous forgetfulness of self seems a fairly consistent characteristic of saints.

Oh, a leper must be a terrible thing to see
When one is beautiful, young, and free!

Young Francis went out riding, upon a summer's day,
His horse was nobly handsome, and his clothes were
    richly gay.
Suddenly coming toward him upon the road he saw
A leper. He halted his horse and watched the figure
    draw
Nearer and nearer, pale and horrible in the light.
Francis had never known fear before, but now he
    sensed its might,
For a leper is such a terrible thing to see
When one is beautiful, young, and free.
There is something gallantly great in the banners of a
    foe,

And the glory of arms and trumpets all soldiers know.
But fear was born within and came out from Francis'
   heart
To stand there in the road, a cursed thing apart
From human ways. Then Francis sprang to the ground.
He ran to the shrinking leper and threw his arms
   around
His fear, holding it to his brave, young breast—
The queens of Assisi's beauty his arms might have
   caressed!
He gave the leper money and kissed him and rode
   on—
But when he turned to wave farewell, lo, the leper was
   gone!
Then Francis knew by the brighter sunlight on the dust
That all the poor brothers of Christ were given him in
   trust.

Oh, a leper may be a glorious thing to see
When one is beautiful, young, and free!

       —Sister M. Eleanore, C. S. C.

From Convent Cell and Cloister

The Missionary

Sister Eleanore makes us see with sudden clearness how much the missioners give up and what bright inward flame of sacrifice warms and makes bearable the last hard moments before they go to those far fields, "white already to harvest."

>Now that I have decided I must go
>I find the dear familiar things
>I had not valued much
>Invested with a charm I did not know
>They had. My fingers, like the wings
>Of homing birds, hovering, touch
>My bed, my chair, my window-pane a-glow
>From setting suns, each of which brings
>My going nearer. Such
>A new and strange delight I know
>In faces framed with radiance that clings
>To golden hair, in eyes of blue that touch
>All things with light, for I shall know
>Brown faces only, eyes as dark as wings
>Of night, shadowy hair. Yet, since for such
>As these the Son of Man no home could know,
>My eyes and hands shall keep but memoried
>   things
>To dull my hunger with a dream-made touch.
>
>   —Sister M. Eleanore, C. S. C.

Resignation

This Ursuline nun makes that heroic virtue, resignation, seem quite easy of achievement.

>When Angel Death comes knocking at my door,
>   I shall not fret, but fold my work away
>   Unfinished as it is, in Time's locked drawer …
>   God did not wish that I should still
>   Do more.
>   —Mother Francis D'Assisi, O. S. U.

Madonna Remembers

Sister Edwardine of the Order of Mercy tells us why the Blessed Mother likes white flowers and why she loves to see little children kneeling before her shrine. She also suggests in her second poem the beauty that attaches to words because of the meaning they hold for us. It would be interesting to extend the list begun by Sister Edwardine.

>Madonna loves
>The first white buds of May
>That little children bring

To lay before her feet.
Madonna's heart sings
When they kneel
In briefest prayer,
Just for a moment snatched
From marbles and kites and ball.
She would up-gather
Giver and gift,
Holding them tight
Within her mantle's blue,
For then
Madonna sees again
An old, forgotten garden
Where a little Lad,
In Nazareth,
Left other boys and play
To bring for her delight
The first white buds of May.

—Sister M. Edwardine, O. M.

Ad Mariam

Some words are tall white candles to honor Mary's name;
Holiness and purity lift high their steady flame.

Our Lady's words are silver bells that ring across the gloom;
Hark! "Magnificat anima mea Dominum!"

Some names are quiet waters sleeping in the night;
Bethlehem and Nazareth hold secrets of delight.

But one word is a lonely rose of scarlet mystery,
Nor all the tears of Mary's heart can whiten Calvary.

—Sister M. Edwardine, O. M.

From My Window

Mother Columba of the Society of the Holy Child Jesus gives us a pleasant idea of how the flowers praise God.

There's a Convent garden across the way
And it praises God both night and day.

An Irish Saint far over the Sea
Once taught me the Flowers' Psalmody.

Each Flower, by its perfume, sweetly sings
Its part in Earth's Chorus to the King of Kings.

When the Chapel bell rings out on the breeze,
"Laudate Dominum," whisper the Trees.

And the Grasses murmur, "Miserere"
While the Roses carol, "Ave, Mary."

Fair lilies, pure as the driven snow
Sing, "Benedicamus Domino."

And the Weeping Willows softly say,
"Requiescant in Pace."

The Golden Dandelions in the purple clover
Chant, "Alleluia" three times over.

The Tulips in their colors bright
Sing, "Sursum Corda" with all their might.

The Pansies lift their lovely faces
And chorus, "Deo Gratias" for His graces.

Each Bluebell rings a dainty gong
And, "Sanctus, Sanctus," is its song.

The Stars of Bethlehem, fair and small,
Sing, "Venite Adoremus" to us all.

The Pine Trees hold their heads quite high
And shout, "Gloria in Excelsis" to the sky.

The Violets nestling in the grass
Call, "Dominus Vobiscum," to those who pass.

The Fragrant Woodbine seems to say
Over and over, "Propter Te."

The gentle Vines as they creep along
Make "Fiat Voluntas Tua" their humble song.

And at night when the Flowers droop and nod
Their perfume still honors Almighty God.

Thus the Convent garden across the way
Praises the Lord both night and day.
—Mother M. Columba, S. H. C. J.

Gifts

When little crosses or inconveniences, tiresome or unpleasant tasks, or even severe trials confront us day by day, we may if we wish welcome them as gifts to lay at the feet of the King.

O Jesus, little King,
Unto Thy feet my ardent love I bring.

Thou knowest that indeed I love Thee well—
More than my tongue, or any tongue can tell.
Then clasp me in Thy tiny arms. Caress
This heart of mine with baby tenderness.
Grant that my life, my joy, my love may be
Enfolded in Thy love's Infinity.
Accept my gift—I lay it at Thy feet.
Thou art so sweet—so sweet!

Behold I bring to Thee
Duties most faithfully and gladly done.
Oh, bless them everyone.
Do Thou accept, sweet Child, my industry.
I offer, as did Joseph, every task
But for Thy love, nor other payment ask
Than that which he received each eventide:

Oh, grant me of Thy grace
To see Thine arms for welcoming spread wide,
To feel Thy Baby kiss upon my face.
Accept my gift—I lay it at Thy feet.
Thou art so sweet—so sweet!

Dear Jesus, at Thy birth
Behold I give Thee laughter and sweet mirth.
Thou knowest all my laughter is for Thee.
Wilt come then, Jesukin, and play with me?
O gurgling little Baby, deign to bless
My joy, my mirth—yes, and my foolishness!
Accept my gift—I lay it at Thy feet.
Thou art so sweet—so sweet!

Silence I give Thee; O Child Divine,
Accept this gift of mine.
Silence that joys to speak when 'tis Thy will,
Silence that can keep very, very still
To hear Thee speak. Oh, speak to me today.
Accept this gift which joyfully I lay
At Thy dear baby feet.
Thou art so very sweet—so very sweet!

Behold I offer Thee
Sweet thoughtfulness and generosity.
Big-hearted little Jesus, deign to bless
My every little act of thoughtfulness.
I love Thee and I do them for Thy sake;
Oh, deign my gift to take.
Dear little Child, I lay it at Thy feet.
Thou art so sweet—so sweet!

Behold I bring to Thee
A little package of sweet charity.
Thou wast so gentle and so kind to all
From Mother Mary down to lambkin small.
Accept my gift—I lay it at Thy feet.
Thou art so sweet—so sweet!

A heart brimful of gratitude I bring.
Thank Thee for love, for joy, for everything.
For dear ones whom I love and who love me,
And most of all I thank Thee just for Thee!
Accept my gift—I lay it at Thy feet.
Thou art so sweet—so sweet!

—Sister Mary of the Visitation, Vis. B. V. M.

The Spinning Top

Sister Mary Angelita of the Sisters of Charity of the Blessed Virgin Mary likes to play with words. Her slender volume, "Starshine and Candlelight" contains some charming verses.

> The earth is like a spinning top
>   With lovely colors bright;
> Through golden paths of day it moves
>   And starry fields of night.
>
> God poised it on creation's rim,
>   Then sent it spinning far
> Adown the dusky aisles of space,
>   Past star on wide-eyed star.
>
> And One doth watch, with love-filled eyes
>   And eager, quickening breath,
> His treasure dear, His spinning top,
>   The Boy of Nazareth.

—Sister Mary Angelita, B. V. M.

Scattering Flowers

In the home of the "Little Flower" in Lisieux one may see her room with all her toys—her dolls and doll-house, her bird-cage, and the little desk where she studied her lessons. With what affection we meditate upon this small saint trying to serve God in her "little way" which so many of us are now trying to follow.

> Jesus, my one Love, behold me draw near
> To Thy cross that I love, in the dark evening hours,

Hoping each rosebud will dry just one tear,
    As I scatter my flowers.

Scattering flowers! Just giving Thee all,
Each burden I carry through all the long hours,
Each pain and each pleasure, each sacrifice small—
    These are my flowers.

Lord, let me shower Thee with perfume of flowers;
Ne'er let my soul from Thy beauty depart.
May I give Thee all in life's weariest hours,
    Let me touch Thy dear Heart!

Scattering flowers! Dear Jesus, behold
How I long to save sinners from Hell's bitter hours.
Thine is the victory, mine to disarm
    Thy justice with flowers.

The petals of roses Thy sweet face caress,
Saying my heart calls to Thine up above.
Each rose gives Thee thanks for Thy great tenderness;
    O, smile on my love!

Scattering flowers! The one joy here for me,
The happiest moments in life's heavy hours—
In Heaven I shall soon with the bright angels be,
    Scattering flowers!

—Ste. Thérèse de l'Enfant Jésus

From Convent Cell and Cloister

Rabboni! Master!

Bethany is the place where lived Martha, Mary, and Lazarus at whose house Jesus visited and where he was addressed reverently as "Rabboni" or "Master."

That He Who lay on Mary's knee,
Who stilled the waves of Galilee,
Was the dear Guest at Bethany,
And bled and died on Calvary,
That He in truth abides with me
I hold with faith's sure certainty.
    O God, O hidden Deity,
        Profoundly I here worship Thee,
            Rabboni! Master!

O God, most wonderful in all Thy ways,
Most in this mystery of love, upraise
My heart to Thee in canticles of praise,
    Rabboni! Master!

And since my hungry soul this day is fed
With "meat indeed," with Thee the living Bread,
Give me to live by Thee as Thou hast said,
    Rabboni! Master!

—Mother Loyola, Inst. B. V. M.

St. Teresa's Book-mark

The great Teresa of Avila, who reformed and glorified the order of Discalced Carmelites, was a Spanish nun with a wonderful power of organization and a marvelous gift of poetry. She and little Therese of Lisieux, her namesake, are the pride of Carmel.

> Let nothing disturb thee,
> Let nothing affright thee.
> All things are passing;
> God only is changeless.
> Patience gains all things.
> Who hath God wanteth nothing;
> God alone sufficeth.
>
> —St. Teresa of Avila

Young Voices

Sanctuary

The poems that follow were all written by students in Catholic colleges and, although necessarily few in number, serve to point out that the Catholic tradition in poetry is being fostered faithfully by our splendid teaching orders.

> The stars that swing from twilight to far dawn
> Are beads of God's Own Rosary whereon
> His great Archangels, night-long passing pray;
> His blazing sun His censer, swung all day;
> The moon His Sanctuary lamp, perpetual,
> With odorous balsams filled, ambrosial;
> And seas and crags shout up with one accord,
> "For Thy vast mercy, thanks, O Holy Lord!"
>
> —Mildred Wojtalewicz
> *Rosary College, River Forest, Illinois (Dominican Sisters)*

A Prayer

Since this poem was written, the author has become a Dominican nun, Sister Albertus Magnus.

> O Thou great Author of the World
> Of woods, and sky, and sea
> Whose lyrics are the notes of birds
> And wind songs in a tree,
> The fluent leaves in mystic strains
> Chant Thy praise joyously.
> Grant me the gift of shining words;
> I, too, shall worship Thee.
>
> —Marion McGrath
> *Rosary College, River Forest, Illinois (Dominican Sisters)*

To Joseph

Virgin calm and gentle, in thine eyes
A mystery of sadness lies—
These lilies on thine arm, Saint Joseph,
Did they share thy secret fears
And are the crystal drops within their waxen cups the
 tears
That, silent and alone, thy sore heart shed
To see the Cross o'ershadowing
A Child's fair head?

—Harriet Hoock
Nazareth College of Rochester (Sisters of St. Joseph)

Stella Matutina

She brings Him, smiling, in her arms to me,
Saying, this Lady with the tender, trusting smile:
"I've brought Him down from Heaven, so that you
Could hold Him in your arms a little while."

—Lillian Doherty
Rosary College, River Forest, Illinois (Dominican Sisters)

Answer

Seek otherwhere for happiness?
But this, O stranger, is my Father's house—
So filled with beauty
That my young heart aches to look on it.
Beauty that nowhere is in all the world
But here:
Not in the glory of the orient's crimson hues,
Nor in the dim-lit lamps of night
Strung on the staircase to the moon;
Not in the rose's velvet heart,
Nor in the throat of nightingale;
Not in the vast and silent sea
Nor in the purple-misted mount—
Yet these are beautiful indeed—
But beauty that the fragile word
Can ne'er describe,
A precious heritage for loving Sire
To give His children dear.
Could I be happy otherwhere than here?
Ah stranger, no! I love my Father's house.

—HARRIET HOOCK
Nazareth College of Rochester (Sisters of St. Joseph)

In Honor of Mary

Angelus Domini

The Salutation of the Angel Gabriel

The Mother of God has been the inspiration of so many poets that volumes could be compiled on that theme alone. The ones here presented are some of the chief liturgical poems of the Church. Everyone knows the "Angelus," and most of us stop at the sound of the bell to say at least an "Ave." "The Magnificat," the four anthems which follow it, and the well-known "Ave, Maris Stella" are all from the "Little Office of the Blessed Virgin" which is said by many religious, tertiaries, and lay people every day. The anthems change with the season. The "Little Office of the Immaculate Conception" is usually said by Children of Mary at their meetings, and the "Ave Sanctissima" is included because it is typical of thousands of hymns to Mary in various languages all over the world.

> The Angel of the Lord declared unto Mary
> And she conceived of the Holy Ghost.
>
> "Behold the handmaid of the Lord.
> Be it done to me according to Thy Word."
>
> And the word WAS MADE FLESH
> And dwelt among us.
>
> Pray for us, O holy Mother of God,
> That we may be made worthy
>   Of the promises of Christ.

In Honor of Mary

A Prayer of Praise to Mary

For the Feast of the Immaculate Conception

>Thou art all fair, O Mary.
>Thou art all fair, O Mary.
>And there is no stain of original sin in Thee.
>And there is no stain of original sin in Thee.
>Thou art the glory of Jerusalem.
>Thou art the joy of Israel.
>Thou art the honor of our people.
>Thou art the advocate of sinners.
>O Mary, O Mary!
>Virgin most wise, Mother most kind,
>>Pray for us!
>Intercede for us with Jesus Christ, Our Lord.
>In Thy conception, O Virgin, Thou wast immaculate.
>Pray for us to the Father Whose Son Thou didst bear.

The Magnificat

The Canticle of the Blessed Virgin

>My soul doth magnify the Lord;
>>And my spirit hath rejoiced
>>>in God, my Saviour.
>Because He hath regarded the humility
>>of His handmaid;

For behold, from henceforth, all generations
    shall call me blessed.
  For He Who is mighty
  Hath done great things to me,
  And holy is His name.
And His mercy is from generation to generation
    Unto Them that fear Him.
He hath shown might in His arm;
  He hath scattered the proud
    In the conceit of their hearts.
He hath cast down the mighty from their seats,
    and hath exalted the humble.
He hath filled the hungry with good things,
And the rich He hath sent away empty.
  He hath received Israel, His servant,
  Being mindful of His mercy.
  As He spoke to our fathers,
    to Abraham
  And to his seed forever.

In Honor of Mary

Alma Redemptoris

Advent

Mother of Christ, hear Thou Thy people's cry
Star of the deep, and Portal of the Sky!
Mother of Him who Thee from nothing made,
Sinking we strive, and call to Thee for aid:
Oh, by that joy which Gabriel brought to Thee,
Pure virgin, first and last, look on our misery.

Ave Regina

Lent

Hail, O Queen of heaven enthroned!
Hail, by angels mistress owned!
Root of Jesse, gate of morn,
Whence the world's true Light was born.
Glorious virgin, joy to Thee,
Loveliest whom in heaven they see.
Fairest Thou where all are fair!
Plead with Christ our sins to spare.

Regina Coeli

Easter to Pentecost

O queen of heaven, rejoice,
    Alleluia!

For He Whom thou wast meet to bear,
> Alleluia!
Hath risen, as He said,
> Alleluia!
Pray for us to God,
> Alleluia!
Rejoice and be glad, O Virgin Mary,
> Alleluia!
Because our Lord is truly risen,
> Alleluia!

Salve Regina

Trinity to Advent

Hail, holy Queen,
Mother of mercy,
Our life, our sweetness and our hope!
To Thee do we cry,
Poor banished children of Eve;
To Thee do we send up our sighs,
Mourning and weeping,
In this valley of tears.
Turn then, most gracious advocate,
Thine eyes of mercy toward us,
And after this, our exile,
Show unto us the blessed
Fruit of Thy womb, Jesus.
O clement, O loving, O sweet Virgin Mary!

In Honor of Mary

Ave, Maris Stella

From Vespers of the "Little Office"

Hail, Thou star of ocean
    Portal of the sky!
Ever virgin mother
    Of the Lord most high!

Oh, by Gabriel's Ave,
    Uttered long ago,
Eva's name reversing,
    Establish peace below.

Break the captive's fetters,
    Light on blindness pour;
All our ills expelling
    Every bliss implore.

Show thyself a mother;
    Offer Him our sighs,
Who for us incarnate
    Did not Thee despise.

Virgin of all virgins!
    To Thy shelter take us;
Gentlest of the gentle!
    Chaste and gentle make us.

Still, as on we journey,
    Help our weak endeavor,
Till with Thee and Jesus
    We rejoice forever.

Through the highest heaven,
    To the almighty Three,
Father, Son, and Spirit,
    One same glory be.

Salve, Virgo Florens

From the "Little Office of the Immaculate Conception"

Hail, Mother most pure!
Hail, Virgin renowned!
Hail, Queen with the stars,
As a diadem, crowned.

Above all the angels
In glory untold,

Standing next to the King
In a vesture of gold.

O Mother of mercy!
O Star of the wave!
O Hope of the guilty!
O Light of the grave!

Through Thee may we come
To the haven of rest;
And see heaven's King
In the courts of the blest.

Ave Sanctissima

The Sailors' Evening Song to the Virgin

Ave Sanctissima!
We lift our souls to thee.
Ora pro nobis!
'Tis nightfall on the sea.
Watch us while shadows lie
Far o'er the waters spread.
Hear the heart's lonely cry;
Thine, too, hath bled.
Thou that hast looked on death,
Aid us when death is near;
Whisper of heaven to faith;
Sweet Mother, sweet Mother hear!

Ora pro nobis!
The wave must rock our sleep.
Ora, Mater, ora!
Star of the deep.

Ave Sanctissima!
List to Thy children's prayer.
Audi Maria!
And take us to Thy care.
O Thou whose virtues shine
In brightest purity,
Come and our souls refine
Till pure like Thee.
O save our souls from ill;
Guard Thou our lives from fear;
Our hearts with graces fill,
Sweet mother, sweet mother, hear!

Ora pro nobis!
The wave must rock our sleep.
Ora, Mater, ora!
Star of the deep.

The Canticle of Bernadette

Cantique de la Procession aux Flambeaux

There are few spiritual experiences in life more satisfying than participation in the torchlight procession at the great French shrine of Our Lady of Lourdes. Against the blackness of the mountain night thousands of tapers glow; thousands of

In Honor of Mary

pilgrims from every nation join in the glorious hymn to Mary, and at every thrilling Ave of the refrain, raise their torches high in honor of our dearest friend in heaven, God's most holy Mother. The story, only part of which is given here, tells of that meek and humble saint, the little shepherdess Bernadette, whom Mary loved so well that she told her the secret of the miraculous Grotto in the rock called Massabielle. The Gave is a green little mountain stream.

'Tis nearing the noonday on Massabielle
When the rock will resound to the Angelus bell.

Ave, Ave, Ave Maria! Ave, Ave, Ave Maria!
[Repeated after each couplet]

A maiden of Lourdes from the old mountain town,
Goes gathering driftwood the Gave may bring down.

No wind in the poplars, no sound in the hills—
A sudden breath passes, and Bernadette thrills.

What vision beams yonder? The green-ivied Grot
Enshrineth such glory as mortals know not.

Oh, fairer than queens is this Queen Undefiled,
Who tenderly smiles on the shepherdess child.

God's angels have garbed her in white robe and veil;
Beside her blue girdle the blue sky looks pale.

A rosary gleams in her fingers so fair;
The fine gold is beaded with jewels most rare.

Gold roses of Eden her white feet adorn,
For Mary remaineth the Rose without thorn.

. . . .

Fifteen times Bernadette kept her pilgrimage tryst
With Mary, the mild maiden—Mother of Christ.

"Oh, pray for poor sinners, do penance and pray!"
What sorrow the tones of Our Lady betray!

"Go wash in the well-spring," saith Mary—"And drink,
And taste of the wild herb that grows by the brink."

Oh, strange! When the child digs a hole in the ground,
At the touch of her fingers well-waters abound.

At Lady-Day dawning the secret is told—
"In me the Immaculate Conception behold!"

All hail to thee, Mary, God's beautiful One,
Who gave to the world God's own holy Son.

The Liturgical Sequences

Dies Irae

The Requiem Sequence

The stately and beautiful poems of the Liturgy were written by ordinary human beings whose life stories are more romantic and colorful than any fiction. The poignantly lovely requiem sequence "Dies Irae," with its austere solemnity, was written by Thomas of Celano, of royal descent, a brilliant student who in his youth cast aside everything to follow a man in a patched brown tunic—a man who sang Provencal chansons and talked to the birds. For the rest of his life he wore the thrice-knotted cord of the Franciscan and was privileged to be present at the holy death of "Il Poverello."

That day of wrath, that dreadful day,
When heaven and earth shall pass away,
Both David and the Sibyl say.

The mighty trumpet's marvelous tone
Shall pierce through each sepulchral stone
And summon all before the throne.

The hooks are opened that the dead
May have their doom from what is read,
The record of our conscience dread.

The Lord of judgment sits Him down,
And every secret thing makes known;
No crime escapes His vengeful frown.

The Liturgical Sequences

O King of dreadful majesty,
Who grantest grace and mercy free,
Grant mercy now and grace to me.

O just avenging Judge, I pray,
For pity take my sins away,
Before the great accounting-day.

My feeble prayers can make no claim,
Yet, gracious Lord, for Thy great name,
Redeem me from the quenchless flame.

Yea, when Thy justly kindled ire
Shall sinners hurl to endless fire,
Oh, call me to Thy chosen choir.

Oh, on that day, that tearful day,
When man to judgment wakes from day
Be Thou the trembling sinner's stay,

And spare him, God, we humbly pray.
Yea, grant to all, O Savior Blest
Who die in Thee, the Saint's sweet rest.

—*Brother Thomas of Celano Tr.*
by Father Wingfield and Father Alward

Stabat Mater Dolorosa

The Lenten Sequence

The sad tenderness of the "Stabat Mater" is a part of our childhood. We always associate it with the Stations of the Cross. This poem is usually attributed to Jacopone da Todi, to whom after thirty-eight years of a very worldly existence a strange thing happened. At a public festival his beautiful wife, Mornia Vanna, was standing richly attired upon a balcony which suddenly collapsed, crushing her. Her poet-husband rushing to her side found under her delicate brocades a haircloth garment, evidence of her concealed penance for his sins. He cast aside his satins and his plumes and donning the ash-gray Franciscan garb, spent the rest of his life and his talents for God.

Wipo, author of the "Paschal Sequence" was the Burgundian chaplain of the Emperor Conrad II, and it was the "Angelic Doctor" himself, St. Thomas Aquinas, patron saint of scholars, who gave us the joyous "Lauda Sion." Obviously no possible English translation can give any real idea of the stately grandeur of the sonorous Latin. No Catholic student should be ignorant of the Latin tongue. It is the language of the Church and a priceless heritage. It costs some trouble to acquire it, but the resultant satisfaction is well worth the effort.

> At the Cross her station keeping,
> Stood the mournful Mother weeping,
>   Close to Jesus to the last;
> Through her heart, his sorrow sharing
> All His bitter anguish bearing,
>   Now at length the sword had passed.
>
> O how sad and sore distressed,
> Now was she, that Mother blessed

Of the sole-begotten One;
Woe-begone, with heart's prostration,
Mother meek, the bitter Passion
    Saw she of her glorious Son.

For His people's sins rejected,
She her Jesus, unprotected,
    Saw with thorns, with scourges rent;
Saw her Son from judgment taken
Her beloved in death forsaken,
    Till His Spirit forth He sent.

Those five wounds on Jesus smitten,
Mother, in my heart be written,
    Deep as in thine own they be:
Thou, my Saviour's cross who bearest,
Thou Thy Son's rebuke who sharest,
    Let me share them both with thee!

Virgin Thou of virgins fairest
May the bitter woe Thou sharest
    Make on me impression deep:
Thus Christ's dying may I carry,
With Him in His Passion tarry,
    And His wounds in memory keep.

When in death my limbs are failing
Let Thy Mother's prayer prevailing
    Lift me, Jesus, to Thy throne;
To my parting soul be given
Entrance through the gate of heaven,
    There confess me for Thine own.

—Ascribed to Jacopone da Todi

Victimae Paschali

The Paschal Sequence

Christ the Lord is risen today;
Christians, haste your vows to pay;
Offer ye your praises meet
At the Paschal Victim's feet;
For the sheep the Lamb hath bled,
Sinless in the sinner's stead.
Christ the Lord is risen on high;
Now He lives no more to die.

. . . .

Say, O wondering Mary, say,
What Thou sawest on the way.
"I beheld where Christ had lain,
Empty tomb and angels twain;
I beheld the glory bright
Of the risen Lord of light;
Christ, my hope, is risen again,
Now He lives, and lives to reign."

Christ Who once for sinners bled,
Now the first-born from the dead,
Throned in endless might and power,
Lives and reigns forevermore.
Hail, eternal hope on high!
Hail, Thou King of victory!
Hail, Thou Prince of life adored!
Help and save us, gracious Lord.

—Wipo

The Liturgical Sequences

Veni, Sancte Spiritus

Pentecostal Sequence

Come, O Holy Spirit now,
From the heavenly regions
Thou Beams of light impart.

Come Thou Father of the poor,
Come with gifts that long endure,
Brighten every heart.

Thou of all consolers best,
Thou the soul's enchanting guest,
Comfort when we fail.

. . . .

Bend the stubborn to Thy will,
Warm the hearts that pride doth chill,
Lead the erring blind.

Shed upon Thy faithful fold
By unbounded hope controlled
Seven gifts Thou hast.

Give them what their deeds have won,
Give them when life's days are done,
Give them joys that last.

WITH HARP AND LUTE

Lauda Sion

Sequence for the Feast of Corpus Christi

Praise Thou Sion, praise Thy Saviour!
Praise Thy Prince with all thy fervor!
Anthems to thy Shepherd sing.

. . . .

This new Feast the old repealing,
Newer King and pasch revealing,
Usher in a newer rite.

. . . .

What is new to age succeedeth.
Place to truth the shadow cedeth:
Radiance puts the gloom to flight.

. . . .

Christian truth uncontroverted
Is that bread and wine converted
Sacred Flesh and Blood become.

. . . .

Come there one or come there many,
Each partakes as much as any,
Nor the less for others leaves.

. . . .

If Thou waver, Thou mistakest,
For each fragment Thou partakest
Holds no less than does the whole.

. . . .

The Liturgical Sequences

Jesu, Bread of Life, protect us!
Shepherd kind, do not reject us!
In Thy happy fold collect us
And partakers of the bliss elect us
Such as never hath an end.

—St. Thomas Aquinas

Psalms and Hymns of Praise

Te Deum Laudamus

For All Festival Days

In addition to the great Sequences of the Liturgy, there are many famous hymns used on various feast-days. Since the Liturgical movement fostered by the present pontiff has recently been gaining many adherents, more and more people are actually "praying the Mass," carrying their Missals, and following intelligently the beautiful and meaningful ceremonies of the church year. Lent and Advent are more fruitful, Christmas more joyful, and Easter more transcendently beautiful when one knows the Liturgy. No one has really experienced to the full the glory of Easter who has not taken part in all the ceremonies of Holy Week. When the bells peal out at the Gloria of the Mass on Holy Saturday, when the penitential purple is removed and the altars are gay with flowers and bright with candle flames after the Good Friday darkness, a holy exaltation fills the soul greater even than that of the Easter Mass. Knowledge gives us power to feel its beauty.

The "Vexilla Regis" is said to have been written by Venantius Fortunatus to thank the Emperor Justin for a piece of the True

Cross he had sent to a certain monastery. St. Bonaventure, a Franciscan, to whom is ascribed the beloved "Adeste Fideles" was known as the "Seraphic Doctor" and was a friend of the great Dominican, Thomas Aquinas, who wrote the "Pange Lingua" and the "Adoro Te Devote." Last, but not least, the Liturgy is permeated by the matchless psalms of David the shepherd-king of whose royal line was born Jesus, the Son of God. Only a few are given here, but they serve to suggest the richness of the Liturgical treasury.

We praise Thee, O God; we acknowledge Thee to be the Lord.
All the earth doth worship Thee, the Father everlasting.
To Thee all the Angels cry aloud; the heavens and all the heavenly powers;
To Thee the Cherubim and Seraphim continually do cry:
Holy, holy, holy, Lord God of Hosts.

Heaven and earth are full of the majesty of Thy glory.
The glorious choir of the apostles praises Thee.
The admirable company of the prophets praises Thee.
The white-robed army of the martyrs praises Thee.

The holy Church throughout the world acknowledges Thee,
The Father of infinite majesty,
Thine adorable, true, and only Son,
And the Holy Ghost the Comforter.
Thou, O Christ, art the King of glory.
Thou art the everlasting Son of the Father.

Having taken upon Thee to deliver man, Thou didst not disdain the Virgin's womb.

Having overcome the sting of death, Thou hast opened to believers the Kingdom of Heaven.

Thou sittest at the right hand of God, in the glory of the Father.

We believe that Thou wilt come to be our Judge.

We therefore pray Thee to help Thy servants whom Thou hast redeemed with Thy precious blood.

Make them to be numbered with Thy saints in glory everlasting.

Save Thy people, O Lord, and bless Thy inheritance.
Govern them and raise them up forever.
Every day we bless Thee.
And we praise Thy name forever, yea, for ever and ever.
Vouchsafe, O Lord, this day to keep us without sin.
Have mercy on us, O Lord, have mercy on us.
Let Thy mercy O Lord, be upon us, as we have hoped in Thee.
In Thee, O Lord, I have hoped, let me never be confounded.

—*Ascribed to* St. Ambrose and St. Augustine

De Profundis

A Psalm for Compline. One of the seven penitential psalms of David.

Out of the depths I have cried to Thee, O Lord!
Lord hear my voice!

Let Thine ears be attentive
    To the voice of my supplications.
If Thou, O Lord, wilt mark iniquities,
    Lord, who shall abide it?
For with Thee there is merciful forgiveness;
    And by reason of Thy law
    I have waited for Thee, O Lord.
My soul hath relied on His word;
    My soul hath hoped in the Lord.
From the morning watch even unto night,
    Let Israel hope in the Lord.
Because with the Lord there is mercy;
    And with Him plentiful redemption.
And He shall redeem Israel
    From all his iniquities.

Adeste Fideles

A Christmas Hymn

O come, all ye faithful,
Joyful and triumphant,
O come ye, O come ye to Bethlehem;
Come and behold Him
Born the King of Angels;
    O come, let us adore Him,
    O come, let us adore Him,
    O come, let us adore Him,
    Christ, the Lord.

Sing, choirs of angels;
Sing in exultation,
Sing, all ye citizens of Heaven above.
Glory to God
In the highest, Glory!
    O come, let us adore Him,
    O come, let us adore Him,
    O come, let us adore Him,
    Christ, the Lord.

—Ascribed to St. Bonaventure

Jesu, Dulcis Memoria

For the Feast of the Holy Name

Jesus! The very thought of Thee
    With sweetness fills my breast;
But sweeter far Thy face to see,
    And in Thy presence rest.

No voice can sing, no heart can frame,
    Nor can the memory find
A sweeter sound than that blest name,
    O Saviour of Mankind!
Jesus, our only joy be Thou,
    As Thou our prize wilt be.
O Jesus, be our glory now
    Our hope, our victory.

Vexilla Regis
For Passion Sunday

Abroad the royal banners fly,
Now shines the Cross's mystery;
Upon it Life did death endure,
And yet by death did life procure.

That which the Prophet-King of old
Hath in mysterious verse foretold,
Is now accomplished whilst we see
God ruling nations from a Tree.

Hail, Cross of hopes the most sublime!
Now in this mournful Passion Time,
Improve religious souls in grace,
The sins of criminals efface.

Blest Trinity, salvation's spring,
May every soul Thy praises sing;
To those Thou grantest conquest by
The holy Cross, rewards supply.

—Venantius Fortunatus

Gloria, Laus, et Honor
Palm Sunday

Glory, praise, and honor,
To Thee, O Christ, our King!
Hosanna, little children To Thee,
Redeemer, sing.

· · · ·

Thou art the King of Israel
Of David's glorious line,
In the name of God Thou comest,
Thou blessed King divine.

· · · ·

With palms the Hebrew people
Went forth to meet their King:
Behold, we too our homage,
And prayers and anthems bring.

· · · ·

Their homage Thou acceptedst;
Accept the hearts we bring,
Who all that's good approvest,
Thou good and gracious King.

Pange Lingua Gloriosa
Holy Thursday

Sing my tongue, the Saviour's glory;
   Of His Flesh, the mystery sing;
Of His Blood, all price exceeding,
   Shed by our immortal King,
Destined for the world's redemption
   From a noble womb to spring.

· · · ·

On the night of that Last Supper,
    Seated with His chosen band,
He the paschal victim eating,
    First fulfills the Lord's command;
Then as food to all His brethren,
    Gives Himself with His own hand.

. . . .

Down in adoration falling,
    Lo, the sacred Host we hail!
Lo! from ancient forms departing,
    Newer rites of grace prevail,
Faith for all defects supplying,
    Where the feeble senses fail.

. . . .

To the everlasting Father,
    And the Son Who reigns on high,
With the Holy Ghost proceeding
    Forth from each eternally,
Be salvation, honor, blessing,
    Might and endless majesty.

—St. Thomas Aquinas

The Reproaches

For the Mass of the Presanctified on Good Friday

My people, what have I done to thee?
Or in what have I grieved thee?
    Answer Me.
Because I brought thee out of the land of Egypt:
Thou hast prepared a cross for thy Saviour.
    Holy God.
    Holy God.
    Holy and strong God.
    Holy and strong God.
Holy and immortal God, have mercy on us.
Holy and immortal God, have mercy on us!

Because I led thee through the desert forty years
    And fed thee with manna
    And brought thee into an excellent land;
Thou hast prepared a cross for thy Saviour.
    Holy God.
    Holy God.
    Holy and strong God.
    Holy and strong God.
Holy and immortal God, have mercy on us!
Holy and immortal God, have mercy on us!

What more should I have done to thee
    And have not done?
I have planted for thee a most beautiful vineyard:
And thou hast proved very bitter to Me:
For in My thirst thou gavest me vinegar to drink;

And with a spear
Thou hast pierced the side of thy Saviour.

For thy sake I scourged Egypt with her first-born;
And thou hast delivered Me to be scourged.

I brought thee out of Egypt,
Having drowned Pharaoh in the Red Sea;
And thou hast delivered Me over to the chief priests.

I opened the sea before thee;
And thou with a spear hast opened My side.

I went before thee in a pillar of the cloud;
And thou hast brought Me to the palace of Pilate.

I fed thee with manna in the desert;
And thou hast beaten Me with buffets and scourges.

I gave thee wholesome water to drink out of the rock;
And thou hast given Me gall and vinegar.

For thy sake I struck the kings of the Canaanites;
And thou hast struck My head with a reed.

I gave thee a royal scepter;
And thou hast given Me a crown of thorns.

I have exalted thee with great strength;
And thou hast hanged Me on the gibbet of the Cross.

My people, what have I done to thee?
Or in what have I grieved thee?
    Answer Me.

Veni, Creator Spiritus
Whitsun Vespers

Come Holy Ghost, Creator blest,
And in our hearts take up Thy rest;
Come with Thy grace and heavenly aid,
To fill the hearts which Thou hast made.

O Comforter to Thee we cry;
Thou heavenly gift of God most high;
Thou fount of life and fire of love,
And sweet anointing from above.

Drive far away our deadly foe,
And peace for evermore bestow;
If Thou be our preventing guide,
No evil can our steps betide.

Praise we the Father and the Son,
And Holy Spirit, three in one;
And may the Son on us bestow
The gifts that from the Spirit flow.

O Salutaris Hostia

Benediction

O saving Victim, opening wide
The gate of heaven to man below!
Our foes press on from every side;
Thine aid supply, Thy strength bestow.

To Thy great name be endless praise,
Immortal Godhead, One in Three;
Oh, grant us endless length of days
In our true native land with Thee.

Tantum Ergo Sacramentum

Benediction

Down in adoration falling,
Lo, the Sacred Host we hail!
Lo, from ancient forms departing,
Newer rites of grace prevail;

Faith for all defects supplying,
Where the feeble senses fail.

To the everlasting Father,
And the Son Who reigns on high,
With the Holy Ghost proceeding
Forth from each eternally,
Be salvation, honor, blessing,
Might, and endless majesty.

Ave Verum Corpus Natum

A Benediction Hymn

Hail to Thee, true Body, sprung
From the Virgin Mary's womb!
The same that on the Cross was hung,
And bore for man the bitter doom!

Thou, Whose side was pierced and flowed
Both with Water and with Blood;
Suffer us to taste of Thee
In our life's last agony.

Son of Mary, Jesu blest!
Sweetest, gentlest, holiest!

With Harp and Lute

Adoro Te Devote

I adore Thee humbly, O Thou hidden God,
Who beneath these figures truly dost abide.
All my light is darkness contemplating Thee.
Lo, my heart lies prostrate to Love's mystery.

. . . .

On the Cross was hidden Thy divinity,
But these veils hide likewise Thy humanity;
I, in both believing, offer my belief,
Praying for Thy pardon with the dying thief.

. . . .

O remembrance lasting of the Crucified!
Living Bread sustaining those for whom He died!
Make me a consuming fire drawing life from Thee
Yield my soul Thy sweetness; let it taste and see!

. . . .

Jesus, Love, here present on the altar veiled,
O fulfill my longing when Thou art revealed—
To behold the vision of Thy holy face
And be rapt forever in Its perfect peace.

—St. Thomas Aquinas

To the Guardian Angel

Angel of God, my guardian dear,
To Whom His love commits me here,
Even this day be at my side,
To light and guard, to rule and guide.

The Holy Angels

From the "Little Office of the Holy Angels"

God hath given His angels charge of thee, that they may keep thee in all thy ways.

O Lord, permit us here to raise our voice;
    And waft before Thy throne our feeble praise,
And thank Thee for those angels Whom Thy choice
    Hath lent our weakness to direct its ways.

. . . .

Angel of peace! Come, Michael, to our aid,
    Thou who didst once chase discord from the sky.
Come, calm those boisterous passions that have made
    Such havoc here as they have made on high.

. . . .

Spirit of might! O Gabriel, display
    Thy matchless power against our ancient foes;
Visit those sacred temples where we pray—
    'Twas at Thy potent word those temples rose.

      . . . .

And Raphael! of the glorious seven who stand
    Before the throne of Him Who lives and reigns;
Angel of health! The Lord hath filled Thy hand
    With balm from heaven to soothe or cure our pains,
Heal or console the victims of disease
    And guide our steps when doubtful of our ways.

Hymn of Thanksgiving

Holy God, we praise Thy name!
Lord of all, we bow before Thee!
All on earth Thy scepter claim
All in heaven above adore Thee:
    Infinite Thy vast domain,
    Everlasting is Thy name.

Hark the loud celestial hymn
Angel choirs above are raising;
Cherubim and Seraphim,
In unceasing chorus praising,
    Fill the heavens with sweet accord;
    Holy, Holy, Holy, Lord!

Holy Father, Holy Son,
Holy Spirit, Three we name Thee,
While in essence only One,
Undivided God we claim Thee;
    And adoring, bend the knee,
    While we own the mystery.

Nunc Dimittis

Canticle of Holy Simeon

Now dost Thou dismiss Thy servant, O Lord,
In peace, according to Thy word.

For mine eyes have seen Thy salvation;
Which Thou hast prepared before the face of all
    people:

A light to enlighten the gentiles
And the glory of Thy people,
    Israel.

—Holy Simeon

www.ingramcontent.com/pod-product-compliance
Lightning Source LLC
LaVergne TN
LVHW011422080426
835512LV00005B/215